The Gift Women Give-a-Way and Men Buy

SEX, WOMEN, POWER, MONEY, AND POLITICS

ARTHUR B. McCOTTER

authorHOUSE®

AuthorHouse™
1663 Liberty Drive
Bloomington, IN 47403
www.authorhouse.com
Phone: 1 (800) 839-8640

Published by AuthorHouse 04/30/2019

ISBN: 978-1-7283-0549-3 (sc)
ISBN: 978-1-7283-0548-6 (e)

Print information available on the last page.

This book is printed on acid-free paper.

KJV
Scripture quotations marked KJV are from the Holy Bible, King James Version
(Authorized Version). First published in 1611. Quoted from the KJV Classic
Reference Bible, Copyright © *1983 by The Zondervan Corporation.*

CONTENTS

BIBLICAL REFERENCES
(KING JAMES VERSION)

Book	Chapter	Verse (s)
Genesis	15	11-16
Genesis	16	All
Genesis	17	All
Genesis	3	11-16
Joshua	2	1-14
Judges	19	1-25
Ruth	1&2	All
II Samuel	1	26
I King	11	1-27
Psalms	51	10
Proverbs	24	16
Solomon	1	1-11
Solomon	3, 4, 5,	All
Isaiah	38	1-7
Jeremiah	14	7-9
Jeremiah	17	9-10
Jeremiah	31	22
Ezekiel	11	19-20
St. Matthew	22	30
St. Matthew	23	23-28
St. Mark	10	6-9
St. Luke	1	26-27

Book	Chapter	Verse (s)
Romans	1	27
Romans	2	1
Roman	12	1
I Corinthians	7	1
I Corinthians	11	7-9
Galatians	3	11-16
Ephesians	4	18-19
Philippians	3	1-13
Colossians	1&2	All
Hebrews	13	4
James	1	13-15
Revelation	2	5

FOREWORD

And The Lord God caused a deep sleep to fall upon Adam, and He slept; this records the first use of anesthesia; and he took one of the Ribs and closed-up the flesh. The word Rib here actually means side. The woman is not merely of a Rib, but actually of one side of man.

When God created Man, the word form was used, which is the same word used of a potter forming clay; but the word "Build" here seems to mean; God paid even more attention to the creation of woman. God made a formal presentation, in essence, performing the first wedding; thus He instituted the bonds of the marriage Covenant, which is actually called the **Covenant of God.** (Proverb 2:17). Indicating that God is the Author of this sacred institution, this is the marriage model, and was instituted by God; any other model, such as men marrying men, and women marrying women, so called, can be constituted as none other than an abomination in the eyes of God. Marriage is honorable between a man and a woman. She is man's counterpart, not merely in feeling and sense, not merely for his gratification, or his flesh, but in solid qualities.

God did not take the woman out of man's feet to be stepped on as an inferior; nor out of his head to be put on a pedestal as a superior; but from his side, close to his heart as an equal.

The Twenty-Fourth verse of chapter two of Genesis must be viewed as an inspired declaration of the law of the land of marriage. This is not only a unity of persons, not simply a conjunction of bodies, or a community of interests, or even reciprocity of affections.

Man has perverted that so destructively that we have the notion, "**What Looks Good Has To Feel Good".**

Adam knew Eve His wife and she conceived and bore Cain. This biblical connotation of the union of husband and wife in respect to the sex act is paradox to keep a marriage together.

Though Cain was the promise one; Eve evidently didn't realize that it was impossible for fallen man to bring forth the promised redeemer.

When we fail to live with the wife God has placed in our lives, and run with everything in the street, we diminish ourselves from God's blessings over our children, our home, and the lives of our children's children.

It is time to let go of our past, let go of the outside influences, the other woman, the other man, the other family, and the other face we put on to the public. It is time to get close to God and obeying His Commandments, His statutes on sexual conduct outside of the marriage and cry out for His help.

The conversion into doing right by your wife, your husband, your family, has to begin within your heart. The person, who can maintain the reins of his or her heart, will be able to control the patterns of the mind. This impresses God.

The problem that we face right now which is a tremendously staggering one is that we, God's children we claim, are not humble enough to ask for God's forgiveness and be sincere enough to stop. We have to keep up something that we know is wrong and allow it to continue to destroy us.

There has to be purification in your marriage, in your sexual relationship with your partner, and in the The Leadership role of your family.

Many have been bruised, hurt, and even offended because their minds, not their hearts, have taken over.

Sex, women, power, money, and politics are all connected in some form or fashion in the perverted downfall of mankind.

Through man's perversion, the Church goes likened, his family, his wife, and soon his position in society and business. It begins to fall from a towering structure to a life of degradation. Why? Because he has left God out and begins to follow his sight and his mind, and not his heart. He has become lukewarm and not fit for use.

Many men have fallen into a degradative state because of "**The Gift Women Give-A-Way, and Men Buy**".

Don't be mistaken, there are some women who have given away their life's treasure to a man for a moments thrill and have walked out on a good man. This sickness has no respect of gender.

Marriage is honorable in all, and the bed undefiled. Lawful sex between a husband and wife holds no defilement. Sexual conduct outside of the marriage is absolutely defiled.

In conclusion as we go into the reading of this book, sexual idolatry has been a perversion from early Biblical beginning and into today's realm. In the second chapter of the book of Joshua, he had sent out two spies to view the land and Jericho. Now here is where I want to start you out. The two spies did not know that Rahab was a harlot. Some theologians have attempted to claim that Rahab had been forced into prostitution, but however the Greek text of Hebrew 11:31 proves that she was a common harlot. The two spies served no military purpose whatsoever. So why did Joshua send them? The Lord told Joshua to do such, because of Rahab, even though Joshua did not know or understand such at the time. The Lord knew that faith lodged in the heart of this harlot, and God will go to any length to honor faith.

Are you ready to receive honor from God for your faithfulness in your turn-a-round situation?

The title of this book is not to suggest that every woman gives her gift away. The intent is, if when you have married, your husband respects you, takes care of his leadership role and follows the statutes of God concerning marriage, the gift is freely given to him. If he stays at home and takes care of his duties as a husband, he will not have to go elsewhere and make a purchase unconsciously for something that may take him to his grave.

A happy and proud wife will be submissive to her husband and happy is the man who is submitted to. It is hard for a wife, to give in to that husband who stays out late at night, is abusive, disrespectful by allowing the other women to call his house or leave messages on his phone.

Your wife is the gift God gave to you to cleave to. Love her, cherish her, be proud of her and being with her.

If there is a problem, nine out of ten times it's our fault. If we cannot get what we want at home and when we want it, we turn to the streets and the idea: "**The Gift Women Give Away-And Men Buy**" becomes a working force in our minds. We are totally accountable for our wrong doings as husbands to Christ and to the lady we have married. When we get angry with her, we no longer call her the lady but a name used for a female dog.

God did not place a peace of trash in your life, if in fact; it was God, and not we ourselves. That is why it is so important that we let God choose our mates and not we ourselves. What God has joined together **Let no man–Let no woman**—put asunder.

We will do anything and everything to get her and now it's time to do **everything to keep her in our lives**...... Romantic Love and Married Love are not the same Love.

How are you going to love the **"Gift God Gave To You?"**

DEDICATIONS

McCotter, Arthur

M.rs. Rosa Bryant (Grandmother)

M.rs Ethel M.cCotter Gillis (M.other)

MY SPECIAL THANK

There are so many people who deposited so many jewels into my life and helped to shape my thinking innumerably and one lady in particular who has stood by me thru my ups and downs, wrongs and rights, she was right there to help pull me out even when I didn't deserve her attention. God will put people in our lives sometimes and we will close the door in their faces, trying to see what is not for us. But God......He will not allow it to happen if it's not in his will. I don't care how much you try, Evangelist Dorothy Sykes Smith, who is now Mrs. Dorothy Smith McCotter. See what God has done.

I thank God for all of you who have deposited positive things in my life. I will never forget you. May God forever bless you? To name my children in their support along with others;

Mrs. Rechetta Parish, Minister Shawndrea Patterson, Mrs. Lateese Squires, Ms. Fayth Evans,

Ms. Alexandria Baker, and Ms. April McCotter, and my extended family, Ms.Melonise Smith, Marvin Smith, and Mrs. Garlene Joyner.

Others Supporters

The Late Bishop Alfred G. Dunston, Jr.	Bishop Curtis Morgan	Bishop Reginald Hinton
The Late Rev. M. D. Gholston	Dr. Curtis G. Lee	Dr. Virginia C. Smith

Dr. Shirley Caesar Williams

The Rev. K. G. Hall

Elder Judy Pierce

The Late Rev. Silas S. Johnson, Jr.

The Rev. Charlene Mosley

Pastor J. T. Edwards

Brother Thomas Wiggins

Brother George McQueen

Annointed Ones Church Ministries

Mrs. Garlene Joyner

Deacon Late Charles Simmons

The Late Rev. W. C. Horton

The Late Rev. C. C. Simmons

Pastor Patricia Thompson

The Rev. Erlinda Dobson, P E.

The Rev. Christina Grady

The Rev. Patricia Dowtin

The Rev. Ethel B. Sampson

Pastor Gail Dickens

The Late Min. Mattie Murrell

Mrs. Geneva Horne

Mrs. Cynthia Allen

Attorney Calvin King

The Late Rev. C.L. Murphy, P.E.

The Late Pastor Ethel Mae Moore

Minister Patsy Cox

The Late Rev. Handy Simmons

The Rev. Raymond E. Price

The Rev. John H. Pierce

The Late Rev. W.L. Wainwright

Evangelist. Dorothy M. Smith

The Late Rev. Johnnie Smith

The Late Rev. C. L. Winslow

Deacon Ricky Durham

Ms. Eileen Dove

Mrs. Doreen Vail, Songstress

Pastor Paulette Bryant

Min. Keith Cannon

Elder. Jerry Singleton

The Late Mr. B.S. Rivers

THOUGHT

Prayer pushes us through life's slumps, propels us over the humps, and pulls us out of the dumps. Prayer is the ump we need to get the answer's we seek.

Life isn't tied with a bow, but it is still a gift.

To me, the Bible isn't a book of rules; it is a voyage of self-discovery. If you read and believe the Scriptures, you put it into practice.

Laughter is the hand of God on the shoulder of a troubled world.

Mountain tops inspire leaders, but valleys mature them.

You never diminish yourself when you praise another.

Sometimes your only available transportation is a leap of faith.

-The easiest thing for the mind to do is to place/push the blame on someone else.

-There has to be purification in your marriage, in your sexual relationship with your partner, and in the leadership role of your family.

We have everything that it takes to make up the "Image of God, but the real power is being able to say yes to God and no to the devil.

Many have been hurt, bruised and offended because their minds not their hearts, have taken over.

Change the way you look at things and the things you look at change.

Kiana Parish. (The Author's Granddaughter)

Chapter 1

SEX, THE BEGINNING OF MORAL FAILURE

The flesh needs medication, but the spirit man is in good shape. If only that was always true of us.

From the beginning of time, from the forming of creation, sex, women, power, money and politics, (position) has been the source of the downfall of many a good man.

The R&B Group the O'Jays said; **"For the love of money, a woman will sell her precious body, for a piece of paper, It carries a lot of weight. Little did we know in today's time we could or would be able to add; for the love of money, a woman or a man would sell their precious body.**

It is important to note that perverted sexuality is not a modern day commonality. It began from the fall of man, but runs ramped even today.

Do you not know that no type of sexual act between a man, and a woman is free of sin, except under the sanction of marriage.

Man has always been and always will be, (the Feeble minded), unable to withstand unless he is God's man. If he cannot contain, let him/them marry, this refers to the sex drive. For it is better to marry than to burn.

From the disobedience of Adam and Eve, to the conception of their two sons, sex has been a physiological function that man has never been able to wholeheartedly control totally.

Moral failure has been one of the most sordid stories in the Bible. Wicked men of the tribe of Benjamin repeatedly raped the Concubine of a Levite until she eventually died. These men deserved to die according to the Law, but the tribe of Benjamin harbored these vicious criminals.

The ghastly results of a war pitting the Tribes of Israel against Benjamin were ignited. The results were horrendous. This is according to the book of Judges Chapter 19:1-25. Thousands died in a total of three battles. In this third battle, the tribe of Benjamin was almost decimated. Only 600 men of the tribe of Benjamin were left. The light of one tribe was almost extinguished in Israel. Wives were supplied to these men so that the tribe of Benjamin could grow and continue. Notice here it said; **Wives were supplied.** It did not say harlots, but every man had an opportunity to unite in Holy Matrimony with a woman.

The kind of vicious crimes reported in the aforementioned paragraphs, have been repeated over and over again in modern society. Intelligence and culture do not change the hearts of men. Some of the most heinous crimes have been committed by brilliant men. Man has a severe heart problem, a spiritual problem. He can only be changed by the accepting of the work of Jesus Christ on the Cross. Christ's death on the cross is sufficient to change a rebel into a Saint.

The Author of the book of judges took these episodes and placed them at the end of the book as a Historical appendix. It could be that he did not want to place these episodes in their proper chronological order so as to not distract from the constant pattern of Sin, suffering, supplication, and salvation developed in Chapter 3;16. Whatever the reason, one cannot leave the book of Judges without the profound sense of the wickedness of Israel at that time. Reading these later chapters is actually like reading about the vicious crimes in a modern day newspaper. Times haven't changed.

We are informed at the beginning of the small book, Ruth, that the story it tells took place during the period of the Judges. If in fact, Judges 21-17 dramatizes the incredible wickedness of the Judges period, Ruth gives a beautiful picture of decent people who love the Lord and want to do His will. The characters of this book are few. There is **Elimelech,** husband of **Naomi** and father of two boys, **Mahlon** and **Chilion.** Then there are two Moabite Pagan girls, **Ruth** and **Orpah,** who eventually marry Elimelech's sons. Then there is **Boaz** who will eventually become the husband of Ruth.

The prelude to this is narrative in a sense is, because it has no positive view of men having women tossed at them like they have no minds of their own.

Elimelech and family moved from Bethlehem to Moab because of a famine. Tragedy struck. First, Elimelech died leaving Naomi a widow. Then the boys unwisely married Ruth and Orpah, pagans. This was followed by the boy's death, leaving Naomi with the two daughters-in-law. Naomi, hearing of food in Bethlehem decided to move back home, accompanied by loyal Ruth who became a believer in Jehovah. Old friends welcomed Naomi back, but she was not happy. She told them to call her **Mara,** meaning bitter. She interpreted her suffering in Moab as God's chastisement.

Ruth went to work in a field gleaning grain for herself and Naomi. This was something the Law of Moses allowed the poor to do. While in the field the owner, Boaz, knew all about her and showed kindness to her. Though Ruth did not know it yet, God would raise up Boaz as her husband. It was not by chance that she gleaned in the field belonging to Boaz. It was the providence of God which led her there to meet her future husband. The prospects are good. Naomi was overjoyed about the developments of the day as Ruth related them to her later. She told Ruth that Boaz was a near relative. In the Laws of Moses, a near relative could marry a widow and raise up children in the name of the deceased. No wonder Naomi was happy and overwhelmed. She wanted the best for Ruth.

No ceremony is recorded; the Bible simply says that Boaz took Ruth, and that he went in to her. The Lord enables her to conceive a child, and she gave birth to a son. The women of Bethlehem were happy for Naomi as well as Ruth (4:14-15). It was a neighbor 'women who gave the child a name. They called him Obed. He had the privilege of being in the Messianic line, for his son was Jesse, and Jesse was the father of King David. (4:17-22)

Sex, women, power, money, and politics (position) is always the center of destruction of man in his weakest state of mind.

When a man becomes puffed-up or arrogant, he obtains a position or status of importance, he thinks or begins to think he is God's gift to women or that he is all of that and a bag of chips.

Success often breeds insensitivity and an unhealthy self-confidence. We saw it in King Saul, and we see it now in King David. The background leading up to David's fall is given in II Samuel Chapter 10. David had engaged the Ammonites and Syrian in war. There were three battles.

The first two are recorded in Chapter 10. Israel was the winner in both. There was one more needed to be fought, but this time David would not personally lead his army. Her sent Joab while he stayed at home. His lack of sensitivity and self-confidence was his undoing.

His Inactivity at home sets off a chain of unspeakable sin. Inactivity led to lust, lust led to adultery, adultery led to deception and abuse, deception and abuse led to premeditated murder, (11:14-24) and premeditated murder led to self-justification.

God feels it keenly when His Creatures turn away from Him to idolatry and to self-destruction.

The Gift Women Give – A-Way, and Men Buy, still controls the minds of men.

God was angry at David, but God still loved David. In His love He sent Nathan the prophet to rebuke him and pronounce judgment upon him. That judgment was that he would have continued warfare and that much evil would arise from his own house. But God's love was also seen when God forgave David. David was genuinely sorry and repentant, and God forgave him. However, God's forgiveness did not remove the judgment. In I Samuel 12:15, 20-26, David experienced the severe rod of God's anger. One way in which he was afflicted was through the sin and rebellion of his own sons,

(Ammon, Absalom, and Adonijah.) Also, the son that Bathsheba bore him died as an infant. The Bible warns us that when we sow to the flesh we invariably reap corruption. In spite of our many human flaws and failures, we as God's people should be challenged to our faithfulness to Him. Be not deceived, God is not mocked, for whatsoever a man soweth, that shall he also reap.

It's not funny when the Rabbits got the gun. As portrayed in a commercial.

Love endures long and is patient, and kind; love never is envious nor boils over with jealousy, it is not boastful or vainglorious, it does not display itself haughtily.

It is not conceited, arrogant and inflated with pride, it is not rude, or unmannerly, and it does not act unbecomingly, love, God's love in us, does not insist on its own rights or its own way, or forces you as men to physically beat or harm what God has given you, your wife.

It is true moral guidance and counsel needed to be given, but the way you say it and to whom you say it, are as important as what you say.

Death and Life are in the power of the tongue, and they who indulge in it shall eat the fruit of it.

Complain and remain, praise and be raised, out of the mess you have gotten into sometimes God has to confound man's **Wisdom** and **Power** to show that He can use a person greatly in spite of their despised nature, rejected or hated.

If walls could talk, it would tell a lot about where some of us have been, what we were doing, and who we were with. It would expose some people's nature and habits that you would be totally shocked to see.

You don't have to be a Prince, or Ivy League player, a Debutante or a Princess to have a skeleton in your closet. Don't you be deceived God is not mocked and He knows all, and He sees all. Sooner or later someone will be informed of your sexual misbehavior and sometimes, we tell on ourselves by our jealous outrages.

We must never be afraid to be different from the world around us.

A person who merely accepts truth with His intellect can remain unchanged by it. Mental acceptance of the Truth is not faith. To produce faith, faith must penetrate beyond the conscious mind into the inner center and source of life, which is called the heart. Truth received intellectually by the mind may be sterile and ineffective, but truth received by faith into the heart is always dynamic and life changing.

When a man marries a woman, she places her heart in his hands, her trust in his heart and her faith in God and husband. When that trust is broken, the whole building crumbles. The heart of love, the trust, and the faith. As one song writer said it so well in these words:

"When a Woman's Fed-Up There Ain't Nothing You Can Do About It."

Love is never having to say you are sorry. Faith is the substance of things hoped for; faith in the heart is the substance, the underlying reality. Faith and Love are the breastplates that protect the heart. Hope is the helmet that protects the head and mind.

Hope in the Biblical sense is a confident expectation of good, a steady, persistent opinion of your spouse, your situation, your marriage, your family, and your desire to be a servant of God and your husband/wife.

First Corinthians Chapter eleven (11) and verse seven (7) states:

For a man indeed ought not to cover his head, for as much as he is the image, and glory of God, but the woman is the glory of the man.

If she is indeed our glory, why do we leave her to be with another? Come back home and abuse her if she does not submit to us after being with another woman?

You have to be careful with what and who you lay down with; it isn't as easy as you may think to get-up and walk-a-way.

Being in a relationship with a man is like living in silent frustration.

1. A tear that won't fall
2. A scream that cannot be heard
3. A desire to be held.

All of us have a past, and whether we want to acknowledge it or not, some of them are **Tumultuous.**

But, there is a way to look at our past, don't hide from it. It will not catch us if we don't look back.

The main reason we cannot get away from our past is we haven't let it go. We still dibble and dabble in the same sins as before and continue to operate in the same position of authority like we've done nothing wrong. That's why there is no power in our lives.

<u>Eleven Aspects of Immorality</u>

1. The man and woman in the garden. (Gen. 2:4-25)
2. Adam and Eve's family outside the garden. (Gen. 4:1-26)
3. A wife for Isaac (Gen. 24:1-67)
4. Blessing and Struggle at birth (Gen. 35:1-29)
5. Rahab's faith (Gen. 2:1-24)
6. Wives and Husbands (Ephesians 5:22-33)
7. Abstain from Sexual Immorality (1Thess. 4:1-8)
8. The conduct of men and women (1Timothy 2:8-15)
9. Christian conduct in the world (Titus 3:1-7)
10. God and temptation (James 1:13-15)
11. Confession of sin (1John 1:8-10)

The book of Genesis is the great book of beginnings in the Bible. Genesis permits us to view the beginning of a multitude of realities that shape our daily existence; the creation of the Universe and animal life; and the origins of human artistic expression, religious ritual, prophecy, sin law, crime, conflict, punishment and death.

The Song of Solomon celebrate the love of Solomon and his bride, who is called the Shulamite (Solomon 6:13). The excitement of courtship, the beauty of the wedding night, the sexuality of the first night and subsequent nights, as well as tender friendship, all of these elements make this book a celebration of romance and conjugal love as God intended them to be.

When God created a Help Meet for Adam, He called her Woman. God caused a deep sleep to fall upon Adam and God took from Man's side; **the ribs of man and made the woman. He did not take woman from under man's feet to be stepped-upon or from in front of man for her to lead man, or from his head to be over man but from man's side to be his Help Meet. To walk side by side with man.**

When Adam realized that woman was placed in the garden with him for a purpose, he began to seek more knowledge after the consumption of the forbidden fruit. His lustful desires began to trigger his emotions and thus sexuality was birthed as a gift to man between a <u>man</u> and a <u>woman</u>. This is why it is vitally important to;

(1) Watch what we let our nose smell. (2)Watch what we let our mouth touch. (3)Watch what we let our hands touch. (4)Watch what we let our ears hear, and (5) Watch what we let our eyes see.

It is not easy as you may think to lay down with anything and to get up and walk-a-way. You don't know what you might walk-a-way with.

The garden of the soul of a man is his mind. This is the main area that has been kept secret from all falling humanity. (Hosea 4:6) **"My people are destroyed for the lack of Knowledge."**

The Garden of the heart (mind) is where everything begins, because it all started with a thought.

We as men see a woman, (not our wives), and something about that woman brings a thought in our minds.

Little do we know she could be someone else's wife, a woman of the night, but what our eyes see leads us to pursue after her.

Many women have been in the same situations. You see a man who looks good in a suit, or a man who has a six pack, (body style that is), and you contemplate what it would be like to **spend a night with him, if only for just one night, I wonder if he can bring back the fire in my life, and so on and so on........**

Why? Because men we are not giving the attention needed at home. Whatever you were doing to attract her/him, holding their attention, you need to continue, to keep the flame in your relationship from going out. If you were singing, keep on singing. If you were going out to dinner, out shopping, continue, do not stop, plan it and do it.

If you were sending candy, flowers, when she least expects it, send it, take it personally by the job, the house, or just be home early one day and prepare dinner. Send the kids out.

Joe Tex, the song writer said it better than anyone when he said; "You had better hold on, hold on to what you got, Some man will have her, (him) before you can count 1,2,3. You see **"A good woman is hard to find."**

We are dealing with experiences here that can and will destroy lives, homes, careers, Business, Political positions, Ministerial Appointments, dissolve family ties, and send people to their graves.

Who is at fault? Biblically, the man, why? God gave us the charge as head of our households and that husbands are to love their wives as Christ loves the Church.

The Bible in the book of Genesis describes an original human pair who is the progenitors of the human race. This phenomenon is referred to as **Monogenesis; the nature of humanity is Mind, Body, and Soul.**

Just as God created man, He created Woman. Although woman is initially created as a **"Suitable Helper"**

It should be noted that the underlying Hebrew term (Ezer) is used almost exclusively in reference to God elsewhere. This perhaps suggests that **"Suitable Helper"** does not indicate a difference of essence, value, or status, a man shares an intimate connection with a woman.

God never gave you property. You gained the Gift through great turmoil. Your separation in your marriage, your financial resources are drying up on every front, not knowing what to do or whom to turn to.

The best friend a married man has is his wife, and you have turned your back on her, and you never involved God in your marital relationship, and now, you wonder why you feel you are at your lowest point of nothingness.

You acquired the other woman that God had never given you, In other words, it was not a spirit – directed gathering that was blessed by God. It was not a byproduct of God's blessing; it was a source of sweat and toil born out of the wrong motives of the eyesight to trigger the heart.

Just because it looks good to the eye doesn't mean that it is fitting for the appetite of a Godly man, a married man, a mature man, or a man aspiring for a Godly wife.

When John's disciples came to him and asked if he was the Messiah, he responded that he was not and that one could only be what God had given him to be.

Marriage is a sacred union and it is not to be used as a stepping stone for a man or a woman to flaunt it with every Sue and Jane, Tom or Harry. What God has joined together, let no woman, man put asunder.

John was a forerunner to the Messiah, and he was fulfilling a call God had given him. We cannot acquire and become anything that God has not given us. God gave John that anointing. We must ask whether we are trying to be or trying to acquire anything God has not given us. When we seek to acquire anything that God has not given us, we can expect God to respond to us like any good father would to a child.

He will remove that which the child is not supposed to have.

David understood this principle. When he was preparing to furnish the Temple, he told God in his prayer; **"Everything comes from you, and we have given you what comes from your hand" (1ˢᵗ. Chron. 29:14b)**

God will use pain in order to create a love relationship with His creation. This statement, this thought, may challenge your theology. However, consider that God allowed Jesus to experience incredible pain in order to create an opportunity to have a relationship with his creation. Consider how Jesus created a relationship with Paul. He blinded him and used a crisis in his life to bring him into a relationship with him and use him for God's purposes. Consider how God recruited Jonah for the Mission he had for him.

This is not God's first choice for his creation. Romans 2:4 reveal that God's preference is to show mercy and kindness. "Or do you show contempt for the riches of His kindness, tolerance, and patience, not realizing that God's kindness leads you toward repentance?" The problem is there are few people who respond to the goodness of God.

God gives you a good wife, a faithful wife, a submitting wife, all that you ever wanted in a wife, and because you saw; **Angela, Irene, Darlene, and Sarah, these names spell A.I.D.S.** you leave home mad, angry, upset and frustrated in the streets and lose the blessing God gave you. "The Gift Women willingly give-a-way and men buy is at home for you. If you are doing the right things, treating your wife the way Christ treats the Church, you would not have to buy it in the street.

11

God loves people more than He loves their comfort. He invests a great deal into mankind. But, we as men let Him down when we fail in our marriages to do as the Bible say; **"every man his own wife, and every woman her own husband."** He desires a relationship with us and will go to great lengths to create such a relationship in order for us to receive the rewards and the inheritance he has for us.

There are three distinct characteristics through the process of the Scriptures that I have observed.

First; we live based on convenience. Our obedience is largely based on circumstances in our lives. We choose to obey based on the circumstances.

Second; is the Crisis stage. God allows a Crisis to come into our lives. We are motivated to obey God in order to get out of the pain of our situation. Many times God allows us to stay in this condition in order to demonstrate His love and faithfulness during our pain. Gradually, we discover something new about God and often have a personal encounter with Him that changes us. Our very nature is affected by this God-encounter.

Third; is a relationship that is motivated now by love and devotion instead of pain? This is where God desires us to be. Another way of saying this is we are no longer seeking His hand we are seeking Him. We want to know God personally. Our life is in His hands. If not, it should be.

Obedience will not last when the motivation is only the removal of our pain. Obedience only lasts when the motivation is loving devotion. If it is not love, why not tell the Lord, your wife, your husband, you love them today and desire to know more about Christ, your wife or your husband.

Chapter 2

LOVE HER OR LEAVE HER

The pain in losing her, losing him, and now the person you are with is not all you expected. Their habits have changed, they drink alcohol now, they argue and fight with you now, and they leave the house at night for long periods of time and return late and go to bed. No communications, no time for your personal needs.

Sex in the marriage is God's gift for the mutual pleasure of the married couple. She should never be **forced, abused, molested, and dragged into any acts she wants no part of, or told defaming things to mentally tear her apart.** Women have a way of telling men the things above and most especially if he is soft hearted.

Sex in the marriage is the highest form of physical ecstasy. Nothing compares with it, and God deigned it that way. He intended for human beings to experience the exquisite pleasure of orgasm, but it is equally clear that he designed sex to be experienced only within the secure confines of marriage. If the husband stayed at home, he would willingly receive the gift God gave the woman/wife for him instead of him somewhere buying that gift or with someone else receiving a gift not his and not knowing what lies dormant in wait for him.

Most men would rather have the surprise of the fantasy of being with someone other than their wife because they claim;

1. The thrill is gone.
2. She has no desire for me
3. She does not look good at night for me
4. I'm in this act all by myself
5. She says yes, but she won't get involved fully
6. Once it's over, she turns her back on me
7. Is she doing this just because, or does she really want it?

Now men, you know exactly why all the above are occurring;

1. You treat her like your girl in the street
2. You don't make her feel desired, feel beautiful, feel wanted
3. Send her to the Beauty Shop like you use to
4. Nights and Nights go by and you are not at home
5. She is only submitting because that's her task
6. You need to cuddle her, talk to her afterwards
7. She may be just giving in to avoid you hitting her or you taking it. Women will be humbly submissive when she is appreciated, shown love, respected, felt like she is the only one, and so much more.

If the woman asks a question, are you my man?

What will you say?

What can you say?

A man does not set-out to hurt a woman he loves,

A man knows a good woman when he sees her and will do everything possible to make her happy.

A man knows if he makes his woman happy and she will make sure he is happy, she will hold him down no matter what May come-up.

A man knows how to keep his zipper zipped. He knows how to resist temptation.

A man knows how to stay out of trouble and he will walk away from situations that might get him in trouble.

<u>That's What a Man Does</u>

There are some mental and emotional causes of sexual disfunction;

**Anger towards a partner

**Depression

**Discord or boredom w/a partner

**Fear of dependency on another person, Fear of losing control

**Fear of detachment from sexual activities, guilt

**Inhibition or ignorance about sexual behavior

**Performance anxiety

**Previous traumatic sexual experience, such as abuse, rape, beating, stress, a fed-up attitude, fear to leave, and lastly a change in sex partners.

Intimacy is a close familiarity that two people share, often with an affectionate set of feelings that are sometimes fading because or due to age, relationship problems, irreconcilable differences, or one has decided to change partners rather than to try and solve the situation of entrenched difficulties.

It is cheaper to keep her, believe me.

Many people think of sex as a defining aspect of intimate relationships, but sex is only one of many aspects of intimacy. Intimate partners respect and admire each other. They find each other interesting and appealing. For caring and compatible partners luckily enough to find each other, intimacy provides deep and lasting satisfaction, happiness, and security

Self – Acceptance

Self – Awareness and comfort with oneself is the foundation on which all other types of intimacy are built. A person who practices self-honesty and self-acceptance of, and loving towards another person in an intimate relationship no matter what form that relationship takes.

The challenges in a matured relationship, however, usually does not lead to a loss of intimacy but rather to changes in the way the woman expresses it to the man.

Zechariah prophesied to a group of discouraged Israelites, announcing that it was a new day for God's chosen people. He sought to inspire those who had returned from captivity to rebuild the Temple and rededicate their lives to the Lord. The message of encouragement involved Surrealistic Visions and vivid poetic images, focused on a reversal of God's judgment and called for a reversal of the people's behavior.

Zechariah returned to Judah with the former exiles and was apparently a Priest. He was a contemporary of Haggai. Though nothing is known of cooperation between the two prophets, they had similar Missions and are credited with the successful reconstruction of the Temple.

John the Baptist, A Jewish prophet at the time of Jesus, He was the son of Priestly parents (Zechariah and Elizabeth), executed by Herod Antipas, and identified as "John" (A common Jewish name), often with the title "The Baptist" or "The Baptizer" The latter probably being the older title. It is possible that the typical Peasant was more familiar with John than with Jesus, at least until after the Pentecost.

The Gospel, especially Luke, parallels the stories of John and Jesus. Both had an annunciation, a miraculous birth accompanied by praise, and a Martyr's death. Both gathered disciples, announced the Kingdom, Denounced the Jewish leadership and practiced Baptism.

John the Baptist unwaveringly maintained that he was sent to introduce the Son or the chosen one of God, who would baptize with the Holy Spirit.

After His imprisonment, the Baptist seems less certain of his earlier identification of Jesus as the coming one. It should also be noted that John had not disbanded his disciples. After his death some continued to preach his Baptism of repentance as far away as in Ephesus. "Among those born of women there has not arisen anyone greater than John the Baptist", however, Jesus's next statement could be interpreted to mean that the Baptist was not yet part of the coming Kingdom.

Elizabeth, the mother of John the Baptist, she was a descendant of Aaron and the wife of Zechariah. She and her husband are described in Luke 1 as **Righteous,** but barren in their old age. When Zechariah had the opportunity to serve in the Temple and burn incense, an angel prophesied that he and Elizabeth would have a son, and they would name him, "John"

Elizabeth was the relative of Mary, the mother of Jesus, (Luke 1:36), but the Bible does not specify how they were related. Mary visited Elizabeth when she was pregnant, and Elizabeth was filled with the Spirit when she heard Mary's voice. She called Mary **"The Mother of my Lord"** **(Luke1:43** Zechariah was a priestly man, a man who took care of his wife, took care of his family, and raised a son to be worthy of.

Biblically it is recorded that Aquila and Priscilla took their roots to be Co-workers with Paul, in fact, Christian co-workers.

Aquila was a Jew from Pontus, the husband of Priscilla. Priscilla is indicated in the New Testament as being wealthy, of Social Status, prominent in the Christian Community.

Jacob and Rachel had a family even though Rachel was barren. Jacob fathered thirteen children. When God finally gave Rachel Children, she had two sons. Jacob ended up working for Leban for a total of twenty years, and God blessed them both. Jacob had four children by Leah, Rachel's sister, but he loved Rachel more. He was tricked into the affair with Leah. Jacob worked for seven years each for the daughters of Laban. Jacob is mentioned through the Old Testament as a Forefather of the nation of Israel.

Society idealizes couples such as we have mentioned, and into today's world we see strong prominent families such as; President Barak Obama and First Lady Michelle Obama, The Late Rev. Billy Graham and his late wife, Bishop T.D. Jakes and wife. After years of marriage, being together, still together, those not lost in death, they dance together, they sit together, and they walk together, hold hands and embrace one another. Those are shining examples for our communities today. There are so many more too numerous to name.

For more people, physical passion and Romance are the most appealing of intimacies, but they, like others are rarely sustained with unwavering strength and intensity. Trust, empathy, communications, and the ability to depend on a partner usually grow in importance over time. These forms of intimacy are sometimes difficult for outsiders to detect, let alone interpret.

You see, Married Love, and Romantic Love are not the same type of Love. You married her because you said you loved her, and she loved you. Romantically, because of your lustful passion, you want to be sexually involved with what your eyes behold now.

What may be good to you may not be good for you.

The things you and I have done for outside relationships to make it work, were done in our marriages, we would be in positions of happiness, fulfillment, pleasure, security, and heavenly bliss

Intimacy And Families

Not surprisingly, families can influence people's relationships in both negative and positive ways.

Children can hinder and discourage a parent's ability to form new relationships after a spouse's death, after a certain age and with certain partner's. Children stereotypically have a difficult time imagining their parents being intimate, especially sexually, under any circumstances and may be displeased and uncomfortable when an older single parent seeks or discovers a new partner. If he makes her happy leave them alone. If she makes him happy, leave them alone. They are old enough to know what they are doing, and wise enough to know as well.

Intimacy And Privacy

Intimacy, by definition, requires private time.

Whatever sense of and desire for sexual expression retained cannot be/ or should not be sabotaged. Shared bedrooms and bathrooms, quiet time together, dinner dates, walks in the park, holding hands, sharing an ice cream together, out shopping with one another and so much more is essential in any relationship, old or young. The fire is not out when there are coals still red hot underneath.

When a person does find an appealing partner, flirting may occur and it should not be under your watchful eyes. The couples are adults, and need not supervision. Remember, or be reminded, they are the adult parents of you, not you of them.

Mistreatments

ABUSE: Abuse can be Physical, Sexual, Psychological, Mental, or Financial.

Physical abuse is the use of force to harm or threaten harm on your spouse. Some examples of physical abuse are striking, shoving, shaking, beating, restraining and or forcing your spouse to have sex with you when they have no desire to do so. Unexplained injuries, seclusion from others, scars, scratches, cuts and bruises are all indications of mistreatment. If you have to beat, destroy her dignity, and most especially in front of her children, just leave. She didn't look like that before you married her. If you want to do anything, keep her as beautiful as she was when you married her or even better.

Your children, your parents, her parents, watch and notice the way you treat her and that realistic love will be evident in all aspects of your marriage and family life. She will willingly give to you the Gift God gave her to share with you alone in your marriage for sexual gratification.

Self Neglect

The perpetrator and the victim of self-neglect are one and the same. Self-neglect occurs more often than Mistreatment.

Look at this scenario. You married this beautiful lady, child of God, mother of your children and now that she has a few pounds from the birth of having your three or four children, she works a job, comes home, cooks, cleans, do the girls hair, help with homework, and you came in late as usual, and demanding everything including sex that night, she hasn't had her hair done in weeks, no time for herself, no time from you, used all of her money for the house and you spent yours on the other woman. Now she has no desire to fix-up because you do not look at her, you don't take her places, you don't even give the family time, but you have been seen with the other woman and her children, and you want her to give in to you?

The Gift Women Give-A-Way and Men Buy. The same gift destroying marriages and tearing up homes everywhere.

The effects of self-neglect can range from poor personal hygiene to failure to seek marital counseling and even to the point of contemplating the murder of your spouse to suicide.

When a spouse has poured his or her heart in a marriage by doing everything possible and with the vows in mind, often times it leads to something tragic. Sadly, the one left to deal with the agony and pain of being without a mother and a father are the children. If they are young, they go to the grandparents, if they can afford them. The mental Trauma is always severe to the point of the children having problems in school, soon to the streets, and into drugs and prostitution. We as Men are to blame for the family destruction and for the life of our children being cut short.

Some of us have spent our last dollars on the other woman and our families are in the dark, no food on the table and the grandparents keep telling her to leave but she wants to give the marriage every chance she possibly can., Where are you?

Husbands

EPHESIANS 5:25-29; "For the husband is the head of the wife even as Christ is the head of the Church; and he is the Savior of the body. Therefore as the church is subject unto Christ, so let the wives be to their **own** husbands in everything. Husbands, love your wives, even as Christ also loved the Church, and gave himself for it; that he might Sanctify and cleanse it with the washing of water by the word, that He might present it to Himself a glorious church, not having spot, or wrinkle, or any such thing; but that it should be Holy and without blemish. So ought men to love their wives as their own bodies. For no man ever hated his own flesh; but nourished and cherished it, even as the Lord of the church.

The above Scripture says, "Husbands, love your wives; and it repeats it more often than; "Wives, love your Husband" That doesn't mean that wives shouldn't love their husbands, but it expressly say's several times in the Bible; **"Husbands love your wives "**it says it because as men, husbands, have more of a problem with fleeting emotions, and wives are more dedicated or more loyal.

Godly women want a husband who bonds the house together and leads out. They want a husband who will be their head, not a tyrant, or a dictator who rules with brutal authority, but a husband who takes the lead.

Man is to be the head of wife and he was created first, but he couldn't make it by himself. We are helpless without her, we need her. God had to make a helpmeet.

Never should any space of time go between you and your wife without saying something kind to one another.

We are no longer looking for someone else to please us. If we're married, we've done all of that. We are now looking for ways to please the one we have found.

The Gift Women Give-A-Way and Men Buy, is the root of many break-ups

A lot of us, and yes I included myself from past experiences, believe that running with every woman who will lay with you is thrilling. It is death defying. Refer back to the story that I told in the beginning. How destroying could it be to spend a few minutes of pleasure with someone new and live the remainder of your life with something totally brand new and perhaps your spouse as well!!!!

If you will give your wife her due benevolence and if she will give you your due benevolence in other words, "due to her or due to him," the adultery and the fornication will not occur.

Honor your wife by showing her that there is no other woman that excites you like she does. Let her know that she is the apple of your eye, and that you love, respect, and cherish her. Make her to feel like in a room of women hundreds of them, that she is the only woman in your eye sight. Don't make it obvious that you don't want her there by talking to everyone else and she's looking left out and alone

The Demanding Husband

So many of us think that Commanding Respect is the same as Demanding Respect. There is a difference in school teachers. Some teachers command respect while others demand it. Some preachers are the same way also. You should never demand respect. If a man demands respect from his wife, it usually works the opposite, but you can operate in such a way that your wife in a faithful way rather than demanding your way, she will generally respect you as a husband. Most wives want to work with their husbands in most things.

Don't make your wife a nervous wreck by demanding her to make a drastic change after leaving the comfort and security of her childhood. Work with her and not against. She will be willing to share with you, **The Gift God Gave Her** to willingly give you and you not have to **buy** it. When husbands are faithful, loving, caring, respectful, trustworthy, and commanding, what carryings on, there are.

You and your wife will not always agree on everything. You may not always be pleasant and easy to get along with, but there should never be a time that you don't say; **'I'm sorry it's my fault".** Usually it is our fault and not hers. As husbands we should make the first attempt to clear things up.

It makes a lot of sense for you and I to ask; **"how could we do this?'** A wife likes to be included. We don't need to go to another woman we are involved with outside of our marriage, to get advice as to how to get in touch with our spouse harmoniously. The answers lie between the two of you communicating together on a daily basis.

Look at the love, the respect, the joy in the children's faces, the humble submission every time you ask I'm not tired, I'm not sleepy, I just don't want to, but yes baby. Humble submission. It makes a difference when you ask and you are deserving of such a gift. It makes a difference when you know without a doubt where it's been and with whom.

<u>The Helpful Husband</u>

Husbands should be willing to help with domestic duties when necessary and even in unexpected times

<u>Look at 1Timothy 5:14</u> "I will therefore that the younger women marry, bare children, guide the house, give none occasion to the adversary to speak reproachfully

This talks about the wife's duties of bearing children, guiding the house, lodging strangers, and relieving the afflicted; don't sound like easy tasks for a man."

If she works a J.O.B. like you do, she deserves the assistance of her husband as much as possible.

If you are off early one day from work, instead of you going over to the other woman's house, Go home get dinner on, get the dirty clothes in the machine, vacuum, make beds, prepare a snack for the kids when they arrive home from school, help with the homework before you allow them out to play, continue to complete your dinner, run the bath water for the lady of the house, your wife, your queen, as you prepare the table for the entire family. Don't allow her to clean dishes, a table, but place her feet in a raised resting position as you return to the kitchen as you finish your chores of cleaning up.

Later, as everyone is happy, full of joy, take everyone out for an ice cream treat.

Come back home, assist with everyone getting showers or baths, and going to bed.

Look for nothing in return by guiding her to your humble abode, and allow her to peacefully sleep. The next morning prepare breakfast and go to work. That's just one of the many qualities of a helpful husband. Your time comes every day when she does what you did just one occasion. After all of that, you expect her to roll-over and allow you to receive the Gift She is not your girlfriend, your woman on the street, she's the mother of your children, your wife, your Queen.

The Understanding Husband

It is said, and I don't recall where I read it, that; **<u>"Women aren't made to understand, they are made to love."</u>**

Are we taking care of our wives emotional needs, or are we just making sure that they have enough groceries and things she need? One of the things wives want above all is security, the security of a loving husband.

Your wife needs to talk to you more than a few minutes. She needs to share her heart, feel the comfort of being in your embrace, and have a date with you when she least expects it. You must maintain a relationship with your wife from the start of your first date and throughout your marriage. This is one of the blessings of marriage. Isn't it strange I can say that now, but when I had the opportunity I abused it like so many men do today? It's not just the young man who has all of the vigor and vitality, but many of the older men who have resorted to Viagra to keep up their diminished extra-curriculars outside the marriage activities with younger women.

How often have you called home and told your wife you just want to talk with her?

A wife may not talk much about her emotional struggles; you have to find it out. A wife may not say much, but you will add to her struggles if you become frustrated at her. She is a human being with needs and feelings. She needs to be handled with tender love and care. **(T.L.C.)**

We as men have the tendency to think that our wife's physical needs are not as severe as ours. In reality it most definitely is.

Heaviness in the heart of a man maketh it stoop: but a good word maketh it glad. (Proverbs 12:25) Death and Life are in the Power of the Tongue.

Sometimes a Kind word from your lips, a kiss, a hug, helps to assure her that she is not alone and that you are with her one hundred per cent. That's an assurance worth hearing.

It makes a great difference what we say and how we say things. Words can harm the heart and it can also destroy a heart, dreams and ambitions.

Don't discuss your wife's weak points with anyone else. Not family, friends, co-workers, or Church friends.

Husbands you play a large part in how your home will be. On the Day of Judgment, you will be the head. You are in charge.

<u>Wives</u>

The wife is the heart of the family and the home.

First Corinthians 7:3 Asks husbands to; **"Render unto the wife due benevolence"** and then it continues, **'And likewise also the wife unto the husband."** Benevolence means something freely given by one person to another for the others benefit.

The Gift Women Give A-Way and Men Buy.

Verse five in the same chapter commands husbands and wives not to defraud each other. Don't wrong each other, don't cheat.

Proverbs 2; 19 says; 'It **is better to dwell in the wilderness, than with a contentious and an angry woman.**

Contentious means to have a fighting attitude. No man wants a brawling woman who is noisy and quarrelsome.

The joy of submission is one of God's surprises.

A wife's prayer should always be; **"lord help me to be a submissive Wife."**

God's order does not demean or degrade a submissive wife. It is a place of protection. If you have problems tell your husband about them. If you have a man constantly bothering you, tell your husband who he is.

It is stills proper when walking with your wife that she should walk beside you, enter the door ahead of you because you have held the door open for her. That is one of the honors she is due. It's not an honor that a husband walks three or four steps ahead of his wife.

The wife's place is a place of power, grace, influence integrity, respect, and honor. We must never forget this statement; **"many women have done excellently, but you surpass them all.'** The Frank approval of your husband should mean more to you than the sidelong glances of all the people on the sidewalk, or of all the other men.

Assure your wife as often as you can, that you are not ashamed of her and that you are proud of her everywhere she is in your presence.

Make sure she knows that she is your center of attraction even if you are in the ballroom of the White House. No one is any more important than she.

The Christian wife should never submit to an abortion. It would never be right to do that. She has submitted to her husband's request and that is her duty in the lord.

Humble authority and Obedience should not be a conflict between a husband and a wife. When a wife usurps authority over her husband, that's when the trouble begins. Wives your husband will assume his role as a leader much sooner if you stay in your place. The principles of submission are most challenging when the husband is not as faithful as he could be.

<u>The Helpful Wife</u>

How can a wife help her husband? In his areas of negligence, when he does not fulfill his role as the spiritual leader? What should a wife do? She can make suggestions, but she is not in authority. One thing a wife can do to help with family devotions is to make sure that household work does not interfere with the set time for family devotions.

What can she do if her husband has poor work habits? Maybe his work habits are different from your Father's work habits. In the same way that a wife doesn't like to be reminded about her mother-in-law's cooking, so a husband doesn't like to be reminded of his father-in-law work habits.

A wife's job is to help her husband. In Second Kings 4:8-10, it tells of a woman who helped her husband. **"And it fell on a day, that Elisha passed Shunem, who was a great woman and she constrained him to eat bread and so it was, that as often as he passed by, he turned in thither to eat bread and she said unto her husband behold now I perceive that this**

is an Holy Man of God which passeth by us continually. Let us make a little Chamber, I pray thee on the wall; and let us set there for him a bed, and a table, and a stool, and a candlestick; and it shall be when he cometh to us, that he shall turn in thither."

The woman was loyal to her husband she didn't pursue this project behind his back. Instead she directly requested it of him. Her husband probably had never thought of this gesture. She was loyal to her husband and her husband heeded her suggestion.

The wife turns her husband right in many areas of life. She has great influence in her husband's life Proverbs 31 say's; **"The husband of a virtuous woman will be known in the gates."**

If a wife compliments her husband for the things he does well, it will help him to see the blind areas sooner. To men, compliments are just like water to flowers.

Husbands will respond to a request in love, but demands stop the flow of love. Love is an attitude, it's a choice. Marriage does not need love to keep it going. People sometimes get married when they don't have love but love needs marriage to keep it going I'm married to you and I choose to look out for your best interest. Tell her that.

Nature makes you a woman, election makes you a wife, but only grace can make you submissive.

The marriage relationship is a mystery. Mystery, or not understanding everything in marriage, is a blessing in disguise. It takes a lifetime to close all the gaps in the most perfect relationship. Grow in love, not fall in love

Chapter 3

SEXUALITY IN MARRIAGE

When God created humans, He pronounced them as **"Very Good/ Beautiful"**. (Gen.1; 31)

They are designed to be magnificent visual displays of God's character. (Gen 1:26-27). Human sexuality originally is set in a context of overwhelming beauty. God's first command is to reproduce and extend this Paradise throughout the Earth. Human sexuality is not simply a mechanism for reproduction. From the outset it has been about completion without which there is loneliness. (Gen. 2:18)

Although the Bible does not define the distinctiveness of masculinity and Femininity in any detail, it does defend that there are distinctions between the genders. Behaviors that confuse the genders are explicitly condemned. (Deut. 22:5)

Marriage and Adultery

Although damaged by sin, marriage continues to be the ultimate human relationship. Involving intimacy, privacy and liberty. Marriage is defined by a covenant. A contract witnessed and enforceable, not just a promise made in private. The couple separates from their parents to become **"One Flesh"** (Gen. 2:24)

Once the marriage contract is agreed upon the couple is married. They cannot consummate the marriage until the Economic Commitments of the contract have been delivered. This is celebrated with a feast. Jesus uses this custom as an analogy for His departure and return. (St John 14:1-3)

Paul commands husbands to love their wives. Nowhere in the Bible is a wife commanded to love her husband, though older women should teach younger women to do so.

Love is the husbands responsibility. Love is a command that can be obeyed, not just a pleasurable feeling over which one has no control. The Model of husbandly love is Jesus laying down His life for his people.

The ecstasy of making love is celebrated in the erotic Song of Songs, which pour out the hope of such marital delight even, is in today's era.

The first year of marriage is especially important and is protected by exemption from Military Service. (Deut. 20:7)

Prostitution is an extreme form of adultery or fornication and totally forbidden. Under the new covenant, this warning heightened by the reality of the gift of the Holy Spirit transforming each believer into the Temple of the Lord.

Self-Control and Purity

The violation of Sexual purity is a decision of the heart. The Biblical concept of lust entails more than just physical arousal. It involves a strong desire for the converting of something that one has no right to acquire. This establishes both the need for Self Control and the availability of appropriate options.

Sexual misconduct is never the responsibility of the victim. Nevertheless, for reasons of personal safety as well as out of concern for one another, the family of Christ must practice modesty in dress, and consider how to build one another up rather than put stumbling blocks in each other's way.

God always provide the believer with what is necessary to resist temptation and make the right choices.

Reproduction, Sex, is a gift given by God to women for their **own husbands, and for his own wife.**

Immorality

Immorality is evil thoughts murder, adultery, illicit sexual behavior, theft, false testimony, slander, greed, idolatry, drunkenness, windling and more.

It is immoral to become intimately and sexually involved with your brother's wife, your neighbor, but yet it is being done on a daily basis as if it has no consequences spiritually or socially.

Relationships as well as lifelong friendships have torn families apart, some to the point of tragedies. Why? Because we have left God out.

Immorality becomes an issue when a marriage is not an intimate, exclusive, lifelong covenant relationship between a man and a woman, where in a new family is established.

Man cannot reproduce with another man, so immorality is highly and truly evident in such cases.

I did not say it, the Bible says in Genesis 2:18. Man's solitude is not found among animals, but God specifically created woman to address the problem of solitude. Woman is more like the man than the animal. In spite of this, she is not a clone, but rather a complement to man

Life any more immoral than a man having a sexual relationship with his wife's family member, his family members, his own children, or with another person that God did not create for him to be with is condemnation against God. I wish you could see through the eyes of Justice this spiritual infidelity.

The Four inadequacy's Within Creation

God highlights the **First** expressed inadequacy within creation: The man is alone God crates the woman from the man's "Rib" So that she is more like him.

Second, the role of the wife is not restricted to providing a means by which to fulfill the earth through baring children. The Old Testament establishes that Human Beings are relational and social and that isolation is not good, quite aside from consideration relating to Childbearing.

Thirdly, Genesis 22:23 describes the relationship between the man and the woman in terms strongly reminiscent of the traditional kinship formula used with reference to family members elsewhere in the Old Testament. A family is traditionally expressed as a husband and wife before any children are born.

Fourthly, The description of the woman as the man's 'Helper" cannot alone be used to demonstrate that the wife's role was either subordinate or superior to her husband's.

The Duties of Man

Ecclesiastes 12:13-14

Let us hear the conclusion of the whole matter; Fear God, and keep His Commandment; for this is the whole duty of man.

We as men have heard all that can be said in favor of trying to secure happiness in this life by the use of material agents; the conclusion is:

It is impossible; the only happy life is one in fellowship with God and the Bible; such fellowship produces the ideal man; any other life is **madness,** because there is a day coming when every action however hidden will be brought into the unsparing light of the throne of God and judged unless cleansed and covered by the blood (1ˢᵗ John 1:7).

For God shall bring every work into judgment with every secret thing whether it is good, or whether it is evil.

Romans 2:16

"In the day when God shall judge the secrets of men by Jesus Christ according to my gospel".

This lays to rest the idea that judgment will be on any other basis; while conscience, may be a witness, still Jesus alone is the criteria, Jesus Christ and him crucified.

I must inject a bit of my personal feelings here. When I look back at myself, and see how filthy a man **I was** it makes me nauseated.

We live in fear of getting caught, being seen, and exposed, but we have forgotten that God, knows our deepest secrets, and He sees all that we do.

Fear can be expressed in three ways:

1. Fear Defined
2. Fear Demanded
3. Fear Demonstrated

Most of us as men who play or have played the games of ex-marital relationship, have not grasped the concept that; **The things that Doctors cannot cure, God can; and when he brings us through them,** we act like He's our homeboy and give him a pat on the back, and we'll say; **"What's Up Homeboy Thank You".**

Saul persecuted the Christians, and like most of us he perhaps said, "He hasn't changed, he's still the same, she hasn't stop being with every man than her husband." Isn't it strange how people can see others, but cannot see themselves? Every one of you have had some secrets. Some of us; did not know how to handle them, and others were a little more discrete. Remember God knows all about us and our secrets.

In Acts chapter 9:13-16, it tells of Ananias's disagreement with the Lord.

Then Ananias answered, "Lord, I have heard by many of this man, how much evil he has done to your Saints at Jerusalem, and here he has authority from the Chief Priests to bind all who call on your name." But the Lord said unto him, (Ananias) "Go your way, for he is a chosen vessel unto me, to bear my name before the Gentiles and Kings, and the Children of Israel, for I will show him how great things he must suffer for my name sake.

How empty our fears often are! How ignorant we are of where our chief good lies, hid, but God knows, let us trust him.

God changed this man, and he became the greatest blessing to the Saints of anyone in History.

Paul's evil intentions as Saul, had preceded him; but the Lord invaded those intentions, completely changing them. Saul went from a destroyer of the Lords people to a helping Saint of God's people. As Paul he became a mighty man of God and it can happen to any of you willing to submit to the instant obedience of God.

Ananias had to urgently and instantly obey the Lord's command.

The Christian Home

Destroyed

In the Bible Zechariah and Elizabeth are the only pattern of a home without problems that I know of. They were both righteous before God, walking in all his commandments and ordinances of the Lord blameless. But, they had no children. There aren't many families found in Society like that today. I like to use two verses of Scripture. Psalms 127 and 128.

Except the Lord build the House, they labor in vain that build it; except the Lord keep the City, the watchman waketh but in vain. It is vain for you to rise up early, to sit up late, and to eat the bread of sorrows; for so he giveth his beloved sleep. Lo, Children are a heritage of the Lord: and the hand of a mighty man; so are children of the youth. Happy is the man that hath his quiver full of them: they shall not be ashamed, but they shall speak with the enemies in the gate.

Blessed is every one that feareth the Lord; that walketh in His ways. For thou shalt eat the labor of thine hand. Happy shall they be and it shall be well with thee. Thy wife shall be as a fruitful vine by the sides of thine house: Thy children like Olive plants round about thy table. Behold that thus shall the man be blessed that feareth the Lord, the lord shall bless thee out of Zion; and thou shalt see the good of Jerusalem all the days of thy life. Yea, thou shalt see thy children's children, and peace upon Israel.

Can you remember the first time you held your child in your arms? That was an awesome responsibility that weighted upon you heavily. It still remains.

That first child is such a Joy and an overwhelming one for a family and the prospected mother and father.

The building of the Christian Home is an important part of the Good Work we may abound to.

It should be important for you and me to find answers as husband and for wives in our relationships before we get married and have children.

The destruction comes when we as married couples allow dissention and the enemy to invade our marriages through outside influences, and so much more.

The family goes lacking of your time, your presence, your guidance, and soon the family begins to fall apart. The daughter is about to become a teenage mother, the son is in trouble with the law, the husband has another woman and the family has seen him with her, His family has no respect for him anymore, his wife is left with the burden of trying to keep the household bills paid, keep the family all together and soon it's destroyed. Why? Because we have no respect for God or the Gift God gave you as a Helpmeet. You talk to her anyway you choose, in the presence of family and friends, and soon the verbal and physical abuse reaches an all-time high. Where is God in this marital relationship? Did you marry her for her beauty and lustful desires you had or did God ordain and bless this marriage? Not only have you ruined the life of these women, but now the lives of your children. This factor is true in every ethnicity and all over the world, we have left **God Out!!** Are we making good memories or bad memories in our families?

Watch me now, therefore shall a man leave his father and mother, and shall cleave unto his wife.

God instituted the home. It is ordained in the heart of God. The home is the first institution established by God.

The Benefits of a Christian Home

Blessed Order

There is order in the Christian Home. The father is the head of the home, and the mother is the heart of the home. Our children are the life of the home. There are clear lines of authority in the home and we should appreciate that.

One of the greatest joys you can have in the home is fellowship. Having family and friends over for dinner or social gatherings. Your daughter's Bridal shower, or the Reception after the wedding, thanksgiving or Christmas Dinner, and so much more. There is fellowship, companionship, and just to re-call good times with the children and your spouse. There is no greater blessing than to sit around the table or the fireplace with your family.

Another benefit of the Christian home is procreation of the Human race. In Genesis 1:28 God blessed Adam and Eve and said, "Be fruitful, and multiply, and replenish the Earth and subdue it." God alone is creator but He invites husbands and wives to share with Him the wonder, the mystery, and the glory of creation. What a blessing.

God expects those of us who share the joy of childbearing to provide for that child's well-being. What are we doing to bring his children back to him? They are God's children. We as parents, as fathers, have to lay the foundation for the family to follow and we shirk our duty by leaving the responsibility to the wife. God made you and me the heads of the household.

"Except the Lord build the House, they labor in vain that build it, except the Lord build the City, the watchman walked in vain" Remember those words above.

Let me tell you what can happen if we learn to obey God.

The walls of Jericho were thirty feet tall. The inner wall was thirteen feet thick, and the outer wall was sixteen feet thick. The two walls were tied together every so often. It; was a very strong wall, but when Joshua blew the Trumpet and **Obeyed God, God made those walls tumble and fall outward.** No matter how thick the walls are in your life God can tear them down. Unless we have God to direct us, we will fail. Unless we allow God to keep the City, we build in vain.

The Best Heritage

The best Heritage that any child can have is a father and mother who get along with each other, a father and mother who love God, and serve God. Yes, they are going to make some mistakes along the way, because we are human, but to know that their parents serve God, to have God fearing parents, is the best heritage any child can have. Your children should see that you put God first in your lives.

No one can spot a phony better than children. They watch every move we make as parents. They know the heart of their parents by their doings.

Dedicate your child to the Lord and keep yourself and your wife dedicated to him as well. When you give back to God what he has given to you he'll make His presence known in your home. Unless you kneel down and allow God to give you grace to live a Christian Life and to teach and train your children, it will be in vain **"Except the Lord build the House, they labor in vain.**

A Mother's Influence

Mothers have a lot of influence on their children. Have you ever thought about how John learned about Jesus? When Jesus came walking on the Riverside to where John was preaching, John said "Behold the Lamb of God" (John 1:29) How did John know so much about Jesus? If you will turn to Luke 1:40-45, you will see that Elizabeth found out the news that her cousin Mary would also give birth to a child. When Mary came to Elizabeth the baby jumped in Elizabeth's womb. She said, "Whence is this to me that the mother of my Lord should come to me?"

Abraham Lincoln said of his step mother, "All that I am or ever hope to be, I owe to my angel mother".

There is not a nobler occupation, or higher calling than a true mother or homemaker. Mothers have great influence with their children in supporting lines of authority in the home. There is no greater love than a Mother who has nursed her child from infancy to woman hood, or manhood. She doesn't sit around with the house in need of cleaning, or reading magazines that are of no value. When a child cries in the night, mother sacrifices for her family. She is systematic, and she is careful with her husband's hard-earned money. She is well clothed, not in men's clothing or wearing a robe half the day. She is honorable in all her dealings. "Her Children arise up and call her "Blessed;" Her husband also, and he praises her."

Responsible Fathers

God holds us as Fathers totally responsible and accountable for our families. We can easily blame our wives, the problems, but in the end, we are responsible, and we will stand before God.

"And again, I will put my trust in Him, and again behold I and the Children which God hath given me" (Hebrews 2:13) remember that.

Nature makes us a man. His choosing makes him a husband. We choose to get married, and to become a husband. But only grace can make you and I fathers, Godly fathers that is. The most valuable legacy that a father can leave for his family is strong spiritual values communicated through the natural routine of life.

The World through Society has a great need for faithful fathers. Our churches need fathers who are faithful. Fathers that their children can depend on. That's the most important need that I can think of. How many of you who are fathers are taking that responsibility serious?

<u>Godly Fathers of the Bible</u>

<u>Joshua</u> said "As for me and my house, we will serve the Lord." Why do we use that verse and forget the other thought behind it. Joshua said, "Now therefore fear the Lord, and serve Him in sincerity and in truth; and put away the gods which your fathers served on the other side of the flood, and in Egypt; and serve ye the Lord. And if it seems evil unto you to serve the Lord, choose you this day whom ye will serve, whether the gods which your fathers served that were on the other side of the flood, or the gods of the Amorites, in whose land ye dwell; but as for me and my house we will serve the Lord"

<u>Job</u> got up early in the morning and worshiped. He made sacrifices and said, "Maybe my sons and daughters are doing something they shouldn't be doing." He interceded for his children. How many **Fathers** are doing that for their children today?

A father is a Priest, a Prophet, and a King in his home. Like the lead in worship, in his home, He prays for his wife and children, he makes intercession for his family. Every child ought to hear the plan of salvation from his/her own father.

We ought to tell our children that we were sinners until Jesus came into our lives. This ought to be something told to your children by both, the father and the mother, and not let them think that we have been saved all our lives. We were yet sinners also.

A family without love and order is chaotic. We live together, we play together, we work together, but the children still know that I am father and that we have order. A father is in charge, but still he comforts his family when there are tears.

Fathers are responsible to provide for the family financially. It is not your wife' job to keep the bills up, keep food in the house for the family, while you are jobless due to your own slothfulness or your selfish desires for another woman.

Many problems between husbands and wives are a result of financial problems. We don't have to argue about financial things. The father is to take the lead in that.

Fathers you can say "Amen" and have the best devotions at church, but if your wife and children **tremble when you come home**, you might as well forget your Christian life. It is that important that your family believe in you, trusts you, respects you and is not afraid of you and your anger coming out. The true measure of a man is at home.

Fathers, your families need faithfulness. The world needs fathers who will assume their responsibilities, and who will take care of their families, instead of someone else's. You are taking care of someone else's responsibility and yours has fallen apart. Your wife has another man, your children are in jail, and the situation is bad but you have no desire to step-up to the plate and take on your real responsibility.

"The Gift Women Give-A-Way, and Men Buy"

Chapter 4

WHAT'S THE MATTER WITH US AS MEN?

We want to be popular in the world, and powerful in the Church, but yet receive the gift that women give a way, and we as men buy.

If we stayed at home out of the dark places in our lives, took care of our duties and up held the leadership role in our family, the wife would be a willing submitter of her gift to us.

You and I did everything we thought necessary to get that special lady in our lives. We went to Church, out to dinner, a movie, picnics, walks in the Park and so much more, because we wanted this special lady because of her beauty, charisma, her superbalty degree of femininity, her family values, or the fact that everyone looks at you with a smile on your face when she is with you. She is the light of any and all gatherings whether at home, in the yard and at church. But now, she is just another woman to you that you feel you can do her anyway because she is stuck with you. Don't be mistaken, because someone will come along and treat her like a Queen and you will be drowning in your own tears.

Many good women have gone down to degradation due to a man who will not love his wife the way Christ loves the Church. We would rather spend money on a hotel room instead of going home being with the women we married. We know who she has been with and where she will be when we come home.

Every time that a married man lays with a woman not his wife, he is unaware of the following:

1. Who she was last with?
2. Does she have some type of disease that she may be unaware of?
3. Is she going to call my house?
4. I just want a one night stand;
5. Is she married?
6. Will I have trouble with her husband?
7. Will she act anyway other than sane?
8. Will she come by my Job, my Church, or my Business?
9. Will I act out all of the above if the situation becomes aggressive by me?
10. What will happen if she becomes pregnant?
11. Will she be a woman of the night?
12. Will she safeguard me and my family and perhaps my Job, my position in society, in the political world, or as a Pastor?

It does not matter in today's society whether you are in the limelight or in the club scene, we have that mentality that if she looks good I will go after the opportunity to lay with her.

Sex, women, money, politics and power are the goals of so many men and many who are married with families and financial wealth

There was a song out years ago by the Ojay's entitled **"For the Love of Money."** We talk about what a woman would do for a few dollars, but there are some men, a lot of them, who have been bought by some older women and even some younger men with financial security in good positions in life and business.

Many of you who are reading this book may recall the motion picture called; **"How Stella Got Her Groove Back"** Some of us may call Stella a Cougar, but for a piece of paper, many of us have fallen victims.

How many of us will admit that you've been on Cruises paid for by the older woman who just wanted to be in your presence and lavish you with gifts, money, and pleasure. These types of activities happen on a daily basis all over the world, by some folks, if they were known, would shock you like a bolt of lightning.

There are other situations that are just as alarming as what you have read. One man inviting another man on a Cruise, a vacation get-a-way, just to act like husband and wife.

What's this whole world coming to, things just aren't the same, anytime the hunter, gets captured by the game.

Unfortunately, I cannot speak for every man in the world but incarceration help me to look at where my life was, and I can say, I was on my way to Purgatory fast.

I have had friends who thought, since he like to chase women other than his wife, I can bring mine around him, and also have him go and get her while my wife and I have dinner with him. What's the matter with us as men?

We have no respect for the lady in our life that God has given us and no respect for the children of that marriage as well.

No son, or daughter, grandchildren, want to see their dad or grandpa slipping around with other women seeing them coming out of a Hotel Room together.

We don't have any morals now days. Why? Because as men, we have turned our backs on God.

I look every day in the faces of men young men, mostly who are in and out of prison, have no education, no self discipline, no real Role-Models, no skills. 65-70% cannot read and write, wouldn't know their name if it was on a piece of paper if you put it in front of them. Gangs are taking over the minds of so many young, uneducated guys, and the weak are forced into special acts.

Many times these young men are becoming a part of the recidivism rate in North Carolina, which is the highest in the Nation at 87.5%

Many cannot read a letter from home, but they know how to stand in a crowd and repeat a rap song. Why is this happening? Because we as fathers are here in prison all across the United States instead of home raising our sons and daughters. We leave that task of raising the children on our wives, the baby mama, the outside woman, and soon that young man is in prison, and the daughter is prostituting or strung out on drugs with some guy she got hooked up with.

We have shirked our duties and our responsibilities as husbands, fathers, and head of households. Daddy is not there to give that daughter the things that she desires, and soon some smooth talking young man comes along flashing money and there she goes. Men where are we?

It is our responsibility to show and be examples of how a man should treat her. This is shown to her by the way we treat our wives. If she sees you running the streets, and coming in all time of the night, arguing, and not sleeping with your wife, you are no shining example. The example of fatherhood and a good husband should be exhibited in front of your family.

You want a model son, be an example of Christ in his eyesight. If you want him to be like you, with every woman you can be with, stay on the road of destruction.

The Gift Women Give-A-Way and Men Buy

This gift above has come between a husband and wife's relationship, and has torn fathers apart from their sons and daughters. A man will leave anything everything, for the thrill of another woman. If he stayed home, lived like a man of God, his gift would be there to comfort and to gratify him in every aspect of his and her life.

A fancy dress, a new fancy hairstyle, a little fragrance, and most men that are not stable in their marriages, are knocked of their feet. You better not forget,

Sexual gratification is for a husband and wife and that is the only place God has ordained such. We don't care in this day and time. Sexual acts are going on in the house with the babysitter, the Gardener, the Maid, the neighbors, in the office on your job, your business, your car, in the park, in the Church office looking out the window, and most any place today. It doesn't matter; society has perverted such behavior as norm.

Folk don't have any morals this day and time. We don't care where we are, or in front of whom... there is a dissimulation in family life. There is husband against wife, wife against husband, children having children, children not going to school, and when they do, they are disrespectful, bring guns to school, shoot up the classrooms, teachers are going with each other, coaches going with student athletes, people raising all kind of disturbances everywhere, and the preachers will not do right, Why? Because we have left God out.

The reason we act out or our children act out is, we have no sexuality in life at home, your partner doesn't listen or respect you, you don't trust your partner, he/she picks on you, and the way you look, you have no outlook for the future, do you tell your partner, I love you often? Do you tell her you are appreciated? Do you support each other in the worst of time? Do you fear your partner? Do you fear your partner leaving you? Do you ever want to hurt your partner? These are all questions we as men need to ask ourselves, and these are things causing our spouses and children to act out because they sense the tension, the fear, the loneliness, and they see the abuse of one partner on another. When a family can see and sense Love between a mother and father, they will be a well-disciplined a happy family and bubbling over with joy.

Do you ever sit and allow your wife, your son, your daughter to make suggestions about what the family will do the week-end, or the summer. Do you allow them to participate in any decisions made in the home?

How many of us show jealousy and yet do whatever we want to do and with whomever we choose?

A good relationship in front of our son shows how he should treat the lady in his life. How your wife treat you and acts around you is an example to your daughter.

No man wants to see a man abuse or mistreat his daughter and our father God, does not want to see anyone of us abuse or mistreat his daughter, the wife he has given us.

There is a story that I was told and a true one, that a preacher preached a sermon entitled;

"He asked her for some and she gave him none"

This was taken from the Gospel of St. John 4:5-11.

In verse 7 of that chapter, Jesus say's to her, "Give me to drink". In today's terminology, he asked her for some and she wouldn't give him any.

This woman didn't know who was asking for the water, but this would prove to be the best moment of her life. This must have startled the woman, because most Jews, as she knew Jesus to be, would not even speak to a Samaritan, much less ask a favor.

So many times, we as men who were bent on being with every woman we went after, would ask a woman who would not even be thinking about running out on her husband, would;

"Ask for some and eventually cause her to give in".

Some situations have left so many in a predicament that you wish you had not asked. You destroyed that woman's marriage and yours, caused problems between two families and now everybody knows because she

refuses to let you go. She lost her husband and the comfortable family lifestyle she had and she refuses to allow you; to enjoy yours.

"It might have been good not to touch" We have or should I say leave some things alone.

1Peter 3:7 say's, Likewise, you husbands dwell with them according to knowledge, **Peter is now speaking of Christian husbands, and not the unsaved husbands to whom he had been alluding to in the previous verses, the Holy Spirit has given correct knowledge on the subject,** Giving honor unto the wife, **refer to that which is unique in Christianity, which is likewise a type of subjection,** As unto the weaker vessel, **this pertains to the physical and never to the moral or intellectual,** and as being Heir to the grace of life, **the husband is to pay do honor to the wife because she is a joint-heir with him of eternal life, the gift of God,** that your prayers be not hindered.

Chapter 5

FROM THE PIT TO THE PALACE, GOD CAN STILL USE YOU.

God wants to use our marriages as examples to our families, our community, our Church, but Society would have us to believe that we are trash.

God did not make any junk; He made us to be somebody. Look with me at an instance from the bible, let's begin in Genesis 37th Chapter and end with Genesis 50th chapter;

<u>Now Israel</u> (Jacob<u>) loved Joseph more than all his children</u>. The name Israel is used here of Jacob by the Holy Spirit, signifying that what Jacob had done as if Joseph was not wrong, but rather right Some claim that Jacob caused the problem among his sons by favoring Joseph but that is not true**, because he was the son of his old age,** this actually means that joseph possessed the wisdom of an old man though so young, and **he made him a coat of many colors.** Such a Coat was given to the son for whom the Birthright was designed. The Holy Spirit proclaimed that it should go to Joseph and not Reuben, who was actually the first born. However this position was to be the High Priest of the family, which in essence Joseph was after Jacob died, the future as we see shall bear this out. <u>When his brothers saw that their father loved him more than all his brothers, they hated him, and could not speak peaceably unto him.</u> This perfectly epitomizes Christ, of whom Joseph was one of the most remarkable types

found in the word of God. God loved his son, and showed it greatly by lavishing upon him all the power of the Holy Spirit. As a result the Jews who were his brethren, so to speak, hated him. Such follows to the present in that those who are of the Spirit, the Cross, are hated by those who are of the flesh. Society would have you and me to believe that the world is a trash pile.

The Lord revealed the future to Joseph in a dream. While the dream definitely referred to him, it more so referred to Christ and Israel, with these men who hated Joseph bring a type of Israel, hated him even more. Thus was it with Joseph great antitype.

Christ bore witness to the truth, and His testimony, and the truth was answered, on man's part by the cross. **And he said unto them, hear I pray you this dream which I have dreamed:**

For behold we were binding sheaves in the field, and lo my Sheaf arose, and also stood upright; and behold, your Sheep stood round about, and made obedience (Bowed)to my Sheaf. It was the will of God to relate this dream, which these brothers would remember.

Isn't it strange that folk will remember your past, but forget about their own? **"For all have sinned and come short of the glory of God."** They will see the past exactly as the dream proclaimed. **"You can see me, But you can't see yourself"** He related this dream in the simplicity of his heart, and in doing so he was also guided, unconsciously as it may be, but still really by an overruling providence, who made use of this, telling of the dream as a step towards it's fulfillment.

The steps of a good man are ordered by the Lord. Are we willing to follow?

And his brethren said unto him, shall you indeed reign over us? Or shall you indeed have dominion over us? And they hated him yet the more for his dreams, and for his words. The hatred that Joseph's brethren exhibited towards him represents the Jews in Christ Day. **"He came to his own, and his own received him not"** He had **"no comeliness "**in their eyes. They would not own him as the son of God, or as the King of Israel. (They hated him)

Joseph dreamed another dream and he told it to his brethren's; and said behold, I have dreamed a dream, more and behold, the Sun and the Moon and the eleven Stars made obedience to me. This prophetically portrays the second coming, when all the tribes of Israel will, at the time, bow at the feet of Christ. (**Zech. 12:10, 13:1, 6:14, 14"9**)

And he told it to his father, and to his brethren: and his father rebuked him, and said unto him, what is this dream that you have dreamed? Shall I and your mother, your brethren's indeed come to bow on our knees ourselves to you to the Earth.

This is exactly what they did after Joseph became Viceroy of Egypt. It is exactly what Israel as well, will do, in a coming day.

And his brethren have envied him; but his father observed the saying.

Even though Jacob had rebuked Joseph, still the patriarch realized that there was more to this than a mere dream.

And Joseph brethren went to feed their father's flock in Shechem. (**About 50 miles distance**)

Jacob sent Joseph to check and see if his brethren's were well. Joseph was wondering around in the field and a man said to him and asked, "**What do you seek?**" And Joseph replied, "**I seek my brethren's.**"

Now this is where the scheme and the plot begin. There is always a plot when someone is up to no good.

Some of Joseph brethren wanted to kill him, but Reuben said, let us not kill him, and cast him into some pit, but we will say, that **some evil beast has devoured him; and we shall see what will become of his dreams.** We see here the ruling of the sin nature.

Reuben was the first born, this meant that when Jacob died, he would receive a double portion of the inheritance; however, the Birthright had been given to Joseph. So Reuben would have had to gain more from Joseph's death than anyone, but he seemed to have a heart that wasn't totally hardened.

Unless as husbands, we have ruined the life of the wife and destroyed the family drastically, often times the heart is not totally hardened. She will give in to an honest and sincere attempt to rectify the wrong in the marriage.

And Reuben said unto them, shed no blood, but cast him into this pit that is in the wilderness, and lays no hand upon him; that he might rid himself out of their hands, to deliver him to his father again. He thought later to come back and rescue Joseph, but evidently he had to go somewhere, but he would come back to late. They sold Joseph as a slave and took his coat of many colors and stripped him. The flesh hates the spirit the latter of which the coat was a type; however, when they took the coat, they did not take the **Anointing, for** the coat was only a symbol of such. After throwing Joseph in the pit, they sat down to eat bread. Their intent was to let Joseph starve to death, but when God is in it, you and I cannot stop or alter his providential schedule. **As a company of the Ishmaelite's came from Gilead with their camels bearing spicery and balm and myrth, to carry it down to Egypt, Judah said unto his brethren what profit is it if we kill our brother, and conceal his blood?**

The Midianites drew water and lifted Joseph out of the pit, and sold Joseph to the Ishmaelite's for twenty pieces of silver, and they brought Joseph to Egypt. When Reuben found out the event that had occurred, the record proclaims, first that he did nothing further.

They took Joseph coat and killed a kid of the Goats, and dipped the coat in the blood. What deception. The same deception has torn many marriages apart, broke up homes, destroyed careers, ruined political giants and hopefuls, and brought down many preachers.

"The Gift Women Give-Away-And Men Buy"

They made up a story that Joseph had been killed by a wild beast and had a servant to tell Jacob. This event; **"appeared to have gone unnoticed;"** but God sees all and knows all.

Jacob mourned for his son many days, this terrible heartache, this terrible sorrow would last for twenty years, meaning that it was one of the greatest tests that God ever caused upon a man to undergo. Joseph was sold unto Potiphar, an Officer of Pharaoh and Captain of the guards.

After Joseph was brought down to Egypt **the Lord was with Joseph and he was a prosperous man; and he was in the house of his master the Egyptian.**

Some eight times in this chapter, in one way or the other, it is said that the Lord was with Joseph. Eight speaks of resurrection; so it tells us that whatever happened to Joseph, no matter how adverse it seemed at the time a resurrection was coming.

Potiphar had more sense than most modern Christians. He saw that the hand of the Lord was on Joseph, and he took advantage of that, even as he should have done.

And Joseph, found grace in his sight, and he served; and he made him overseer over the house, and all that he had put in his hand.

The Lord was in all of this, even though Joseph did not know what the future held; he maintained his faith in the Lord. Thereby walking in faith and not by sight had Joseph done; otherwise the Lord could not have blessed him. We want to act on our own instead of allowing God to work in our favor for every situation he has ordained.

Many Christians forfeit blessings, simply because they refuse to humble themselves before the Lord. Joseph could easily have grown bitter, until the bitterness overtook him, but he put it all in the hands of his Lord, even as we must do.

Joseph was a Godly man and well favored. He was impeccably honest and as well, very handsome.

Tradition says that Zuleikah was her name; she was at first the most virtuous of women, but when she saw Joseph, she was so affected, she lost all self-control, and became a slave to her passions. It is said that she made a dinner inviting forty of the most beautiful women in Egypt who when they saw Joseph, were so moved with admiration that they exclaimed with one accord that he must be an angel.

The devil really knows how to throw a party and who to invite to tear down the moral character and the Christ-likeness of a man or a woman. He has all of the tricks of the game to lure you into a state of degradation. It's all in the name of love.

And it came to pass after these things, that the Master's wife cast her eyes upon Joseph, and she asks, lie with Me?

But Joseph refused and said unto his Master's wife, behold my master trusts me with all that is in the house and he has committed all that he has to my hands.

The action of Joseph in resisting this temptation pressed upon him showed him to be the true first born.

There is none greater in this house than I; neither has he kept back anything from me but you, because you are his wife: how then can I do this great wickedness, and sin against God?

There are three reasons why Joseph was against this wrongdoing.

1. **His gratitude to his master, who had put everything into his hand;**
2. **Respect for the woman, seeing that she was Potiphar's wife; and**
3. **The fear of God**

Day by day she continued to press Joseph and he continues to resist.

And she caught him by his garment saying lie with me; and he left his garment in her hand, and fled.

Joseph was wrongly accused of rape that he did not commit but he ran to get away leaving his garment.

The devil will surmise that if he cannot get Joseph to do that which is wrong, he will have him locked up in prison for years, of course the Lord could have stopped all of this; however he has to allow us to experience some things so we will know he is a God who can solve anything. The trap has now sprung and the master is kindled with anger.

Joseph exchanged a Palace for a Prison. But the Lord was with Joseph and showed him mercy in prison as he had in the palace. This was Joseph's training ground. Would he pass the test? In fact he would pass with flying colors.

You got to go through what you're going thru, but wait until he brings you out. Those are the words of a song, and how true they are.

Joseph never complained, was never bitter, he just left it all up to the Lord. You are somebody if you are in prison as Joseph was, and the Butler and the Baker came to him to interpret their dreams.

Pharaoh had to come to Joseph for interpretation of his dream. Through all of this Joseph still gave God the Glory.

Joseph went from prison back to the Palace as Viceroy. This is a clear indication that God can use any situation we are in or have been in to turn our lives around and even our marital misconduct if we give it all to him. He was blessed with Asenath his wife, and his two sons, Manasseh an Ephraim.

It doesn't take a rocket scientist to see that God blessed Joseph in spite of his being in Prison, he even had favor there. God blessed him to live one hundred and ten years. He lived in Egypt 93 years and his father's descendants for 215 years. This man who was sold as a slave into Egypt became a Viceroy of the most powerful and richest nation on the face of the earth. He was without a doubt one of the most beautiful types of Christ who ever lived.

Your Marital situation may be going through turmoil right about now, but if you have faith in God like Joseph had, and in spite of the circumstances, keep the faith, don't get bitter, God will see you through.

You may have to go through something in order to make your marriage work, but if you are willing to stand the test, be faithful; God will see you through it all.

It's not going to be easy; it's not going to be smooth. The way is going to be hard and you may even want to give up. You have to hang in there if she is worth you fighting for. What God has joined together, let no man put asunder.

Stand by your man, stand by your woman. Your family is depending upon you both to nourish them in love, security, happiness, spirituality, precepts and examples, as well as sharing family values.

If you've been through the wringer, don't allow yourself to be wrung again. Turn your life around and be the man of God your family needs you to be.

It doesn't matter whether you've been in and out of Prison, jail, the crack house, on the street corner, or in and out of this woman's house, or that man's house, God gives us free will to come to him at any time.

When you are at your lowest, in the muck and miry clay of despair that's when he can clean us up, turn us into a blessing, and pull us out of the messing around and deceit.

Take a look at what he did for Gomer. She was a beautiful woman, the attraction of every man's eye, and Hosea tried his best to keep others away from his gift God gave Gomer to share with **her husband.**

Hosea thought that if Gomer became pregnant, that others would not look at her. Lo, and behold, it didn't stop, it got worse. Not only did she get pregnant, but the scripture says that she had two sons, and Hosea found out that neither one was his. He still remained a faithful father, and over the years Gomer's beauty faded. She no longer had long silky beautiful hair, now it was gray. The beauty had fallen by the way side.

When you love her, when you love him, none of that matters. Hosea went down to the auction block and when his eyes made contact with those of Gomer, love told him to **"take her back"** One can only imagine or guess the hurt that filled Hosea's heart as he stood before Gomer. She was no doubt dressed in rags and had been reduced by abuse to less than a slave.

When a man gets a woman from another situation, the first thing he does after he has used her up, she no longer looks good, he tells her, **"I don't want you anymore, go on back to your husband."** She probably reasoned in her mind, **how can he love me after all this?"** Why? Because 800 years later one hung on the cross, which had also been bought for thirty pieces of silver, the price of a slave.

When the love is real you cannot turn your back unless it's violent or physical abuse. God has a way of allowing the enemy to take us through some things to show our love for him.

You have to be man enough to avoid the temptation of another man or woman. The Devil comes **"As a roaring Lion, walks about seeking whom he may devour" Peter 5:8**

The songwriter Betty Wright, from the sixties and seventies, wrote a song entitled "**The Cleanup Woman"**. In that song she talked about the cleanup woman, she rally cleans-up.

Every time you think he's no good, you throw him out in the street, along comes the clean-up woman every single time, and most of the time you know who she is. Your friend or one of your family members.

In the same manner you may throw her out of your life, but there's a song for that also by Johnnie Taylor: **"It's Cheaper to Keep Her"**

If there are children and they live at home, you know who will be living in the house and who will be paying child support and alimony, you.

If you don't want her, then don't wine and dine her until you get tired of her and then run-out with another who will not be there for you when the times get hard, when you have no money when your health has failed you, when you lose your hair, you have dentures now, you no longer drive a Cadillac but a Ford pick-up.

The late Percy Sledge made it clearer than anyone on this subject of men loving a woman. This song was written in 1969 **"When a Man Loves a Woman"**

What a topic and when a man loves a woman, whether she's his or not he can't keep his mind on nothing else, he'll tell the world about the good thing he found. If she is bad he can see it, turn his back on his best friend if he put her down.

A woman and her gift have led so many men from being viewed in the public eye as a man of high statute to the lowest degree of respect in today's Society. Why? Because he can't keep his mind on nothing else. He has left God out, he has left his family out, he has left his business, his job, his ministry his position of trust has gone down the drain. We cannot afford to leave God out of anything we are in.

"The Gift Women Give-A-Way and Men Buy" The most powerful alluding and alluring tool the devil has against mankind.

For the love of money, people will steal from their own mother, for the love of money people will rob their own brother, but for the love of a woman a man will take a life, even his own for the woman who has that kind of hold on him. Some will even take the life of the woman if he feels that she is about to leave him for another man. You know the old saying, **"If I can't have you, nobody else will"**

When a man's mind has become so weak that he has reached that point, he is operating on his own and not with the help of Christ. I can use the term I gained years ago: **"His mind is sleeping, but He's wide awake"**

It's important for us to know and to remember God placed into our lives a wife to love as Christ loves the Church. Do you tear the Church down? The heart that is? Do you condemn the building because it has a leak? The answer is no, you repair the problems and continue to live and worship in that Edifice. A marriage to a real Christian woman is the same way. When problems arise you fix it by communicating in love and consideration for one another. She is not a dog to be stepped on or a child to be screamed at. She should not be afraid to voice her honest opinion with you about what is wrong in your marriage.

Women you are just as guilty as well. Some talk to their husbands like he's the child and often times in front of the children who have no respect for him. She has him wrapped around her finger because of the gift you have that you withhold from him when he doesn't do as you say.

Trouble begins when the above happens and out into the night he goes and before he realizes it, he has bought time with another woman. What do you mean he has bought tie? Ok, glad you asked.

If he pays for dinner, pays a household bill, or more for a moment of pleasure, with a woman not his wife he has fallen within the realm of the title of this book.

Many are guilty of just helping a female friend out and before long; you have become intimate in exchange for all of the cash you have invested in this situation which is now an affair.

Where do you go from Here?

A Woman wants to feel;

1. Belonging and a sense of reliable alliance, that she can depend and rely upon the other person;
2. Emotional intergration and stability, the sense that you and she can use each other as a sounding board, you will listen to me when he would not, and we will do so until the Gift has been received and off we go to the next;
3. Opportunity for communication about ourselves, the belief that we can talk freely and open about our opinions and values and be able to ventilate about matters important to her,
4. Provision of assistance and physical support, the belief that the other person will share tasks that are to difficult to do alone;
5. The reassurance of worth and value, the faith and belief that the other person genuinely cares for and values the relationship or affair;
6. Opportunity to help others, the chance to feel good by helping, or supporting someone who is down on their luck or opinion of themselves;
7. Personality support obtaining gestures of support and approval for the way we do things and feel about things. A little attention, a good listener, a humorous person, well-informed, neat in appearance and dress, goes a long ways with a man or a woman.

Those seven things that I have just mentioned above do not mean that someone is attracted or interested in getting with you, sometimes a kind word might be just what a woman or a man needs to get his or her mind off of suicide or going home with the intent to kill the entire household.

Many men are attracted to slim women, but there are those who are highly attracted to plump women. Every man has his own preference, yet there are those who are attracted to all women.

A relationship, an affair begins with mutual attraction most of the time. You see me and I see you, and now I decide to say something to you and the attractions build.

Why does it have to develop into an intimate situation instead of a Christian friendship? Because of the nature of man. Folk don't have any morals now days. A man will be with someone in his family if she allows him to do so. A woman will be with her brother if her hormones are out of whack.

"The Gift Women Give A-Way and Men Buy

Chapter 6

TWO LOVERS AND I
AIN'T ASHAMED

Scientific Knowledge

The Nature of Relationship

We have all experience a wide range of Relationships in our lives, and some more than others. For most of us, these relationships form the very core of our existence.

The relationship between the sexes is especially fascinating; Artists, Lyricist, and Scientist **Alike, have speculated endlessly about its meaning and its ramifications.** Philosophers, Theologians, Psychologists, Sociologists, Historians, and Demographers have not been immune to its mystery.

Needs to actualize	Self
One's full potential	**Actualization**
Basic Psychological	**Status, Esteem**
Needs	**Love Affection**
Basic	**Safety**
Physical	**Security**
Needs	**Food, Water, Sex, Pain,**
	Avoidance

Motivation and Personality traits are the hinges of this triangle Relationship.

As complex, and varied, and sometimes puzzling, as our relationships are, they may be conceptualized as falling in two major types;

(1) **Secondary Relationships and;**
(2) **Primary Relationships.** Both are essential for the survival well-being of the individuals in today's society.

Our everyday encounters with other Human beings are a continual and related interaction. This is a secondary relationship.

A Secondary Relationship is an interaction with someone we do not know at all or know very little of. Often times this triggers a Primary relationship, or in other words, an affair with someone other than your wife or your husband. Each person in a Secondary Relationship is important to the other only because of the function each fulfills for the other. This function, the provision or exchange of goods or services, is the basis of most social interactions in our Society today, no matter the intent or purpose behind the interaction.

Secondary Relationships are relatively brief, formal, and impersonal. They are generally based on a maturely agreed-upon reciprocity of exchange or **"Something for Something"** For example a shopper who goes into a super market to buy a gallon of milk has a Secondary Relationship with the checker. Neither the Shopper nor the Checker is important to the other as a unique individual; each is interchangeable The Shopper could be replaced by another shopper or the Checker by another Checker without making any meaningful differences to the transaction.

In contrast, A Primary Relationship is relatively enduring, informal and personal. The values each person provides for the other and receives from the other are not precisely fixed and maybe intangible. The exchange of satisfaction depends on the unique qualities each has as an individual. The human values of affection, acceptance, compassion, and understanding are not only important, but also essential to the transaction in a Primary

Relationship. Because the unique quality of each person is crucial, individuals are not interchangeable in Primary Relationships.

The satisfactions exchanged in a Secondary Relationship are **extrinsic** and chiefly **intrinsic,** pleasure in and out of itself in a primary relationship.

Sometimes it starts out to be a friendly gesture on both parts, and someone will want to pursue it further. Why? Because of the sin nature of man that has filtered down through generation after generation and has a high degree of the world's marital problem hay-wire today.

Just as any transaction usually has some elements of Intrinsic and Extrinsic satisfaction for both participants, so does any relationship normally fall between the two extremes of Secondary and Primary Relationships.

If a woman or a man reciprocates their interest and responds positive to the overtures of the opposite sex, the friendship may become a relationship to continue to move toward a Primary Relationship, thus birthing sin into a situation already wrong before it goes any further.

The Situation can take an opposite direction in some cases where a married couple is meeting at a Divorce Lawyer's office to discuss a settlement distribution of property, or custody of children.

It is so easy for a simple conversation, a cup of coffee, the holding of an umbrella over the ladies head, a stop to assist with a car problem, and so on and so on to lead to;

"The Gift Women Give-A-Way and Men Buy"

Lives, cars, homes, and positions are torn to shreds for a few moments thrill and we are unconscious of how many people fall with us when this happens.

Businesses, Political careers, Ministries, children, and oftentimes, one will take their life after such a fall.

The Nature of Love

Love is the ultimate experience of pair bonding when the attraction is mutual. Given one wish, most people would wish to be loved.

When a couple are in love, seriously Christianly, each values the other and is pre-occupied with feelings through dreams, and fantasies about the other; each is comfortable and satisfied in the other's presence and uneasy in the other's absence; each feels that it would be impossible to become romantically attracted to anyone else.

If one of the couple is romantically attracted to someone else, he or she usually feels guilty or disloyal; such an attraction carries the idea of cheating in our society.

Let it be noted, some men have no compunctions, some women have no compunction, or feel no guild, about being in love with more than one person at a time. Instead of believing that this is disloyal, a breach of trust or commitment they believe that it is a normal and expected part of Romantic Love.

Many studies indicate that the need to experience pair bonding, love, and intimacy is a basic drive for most people in our society.

Breadth of Intimacy is measured by the number of activities, beliefs, and interests a couple share.

Openness in Intimacy is measured by the extent of self-disclosure in the relationship. The more we are able and willing to disclose to our partner, our innermost thoughts and feelings, the greater the openness. Because openness leaves us vulnerable to rejection we may find this aspect of Intimacy very threatening. If we remain guarded or cautious keeping the normal social safeguard in place, we cannot achieve openness in an intimate relationship, whatever its breadth.

The Depth of Intimacy is a measure of how important each person is to the other and how committed they are. When depth is a major characteristic of an intimate relationship, just being together results in both people reeling a sense of well-being often described as a sense of wholeness or completeness. When the depth of intimacy is very great each member of the couple experience a sense of uniting with the other.

In other words, when you know God has given you an Angel, a Woman of God, a man of God, and you have broken the bonds of trust and loyalty, it is so hard to face yourself in the mirror and go about your everyday activities. If the guilt is sincere, in some rare cases, the individuals re-ignite with a higher degree of intensity in their marital relationship, family life, and respect for one another. Whenever we pursue the attainment of love, sex, marriage, and a family of our own, in whatever forms these may take, it is imperative that we do so within a social setting. Everyone wants to see it.

Culture varies considerably from one society to another. Culture encompasses all the **thoughts beliefs, customs, laws, Mors, values, religious observance, festivals, food preferences, languages, art, entertainments, songs, dramas, literature, tools, implements, artifacts, and social institutions** that are current in a society such as we live in today.

Patterns of dating, romantic love, sexual behavior and male – female are all culturally determined. They differ markedly not only from one society to another, but also within each **Sub-Society** of the society at large.

As members of Society, we are indoctrinated into its culture by a process of Socialization or cultural conditioning. Socialization is inescapable, and essential for survival in any society. The process of socialization starts in infancy. By the time children are about five years old they are usually well socialized, or indoctrinated into the speech, expectations, and patterns of behavior characteristic of the; society

Social Class

Many aspects of how we date, marry, relate to spouses, divorce, and remarry, differ from one social class to another. Social class is a convenience. Though imperfect, the measure of a person's position in the hierarchy of a society, he or she is always being viewed. Family name, position, church status, and status in the community is a basic determinant in a society, cate system, and has been largely replaced by our, **income and it's source, our level of education, and the nature and location of our residence.**

God is not interested in our social economical statue or our status quo in society. He is looking for a man to love his wife the way Christ loved the Church.

Being deeply loved by someone gives you strength, while loving someone deeply gives you courage. That's the many faces of love. A real love.

The Varieties of Love within a Couple

The Six Stages

Romantic Love

Sexual Love

Passionate Love

Compassionate Love

Unselfish Love

Infatuation

As we have seen in life early, the emotion of love is first experienced in infancy as a result of receiving love, and nurturance from one's mother.

A child who has been characterized by self-love is able to love others. They may learn to love an inanimate object, such as a blanket, doll, stuffed toy, that provides warmth.

A person who has failed to develop self-love in infancy and early childhood will typically become greedy, egocentric, or-self-centered. Is that why we cannot be true to the words of the poem?

How many of us have said the following?

<u>Love and Attachment</u>

Most Scientist accept the attachment theory as an explanation for the origin of love. **(Hartfield and Rapson 1994)** according to the attachment theory, we fall in love when an **attachment** bond of some strength is formed and we stay in love by maintaining this bond of attachment.

Then, why do we as men, we get mad, when we cannot get what we want at home, when we want it, go to the other woman? It's because we do not love that wife the way Christ loves the Church, he never ran out on Israel, nor did he forsake her.

A pretty face, a coca cola bottle shape, a little perfume, we will leave a good woman for a moments thrill not knowing what the end will be.

The Attachment theory postulates that the essence of love is a partner responding to a need, even when he or she may not feel like it at the time. Sometimes you have to even when you don't want to, because your body is his, and his body is yours. If he, if she, is meeting the standards for submission, willingly do so If those standards are at odds, you have a right to say no.

Most of us need to feel that somebody is emotionally there for us, that we can make contact with another person who will respond, particularly if we are in need. Lovers have an immutable longing for contact. They seem to have a desperate need to connect.

The person who is attached to another feels a sense of warmth, comfort, and security when the other is felt to be accessible and responsive and a sense of **separation distress** when the other is felt to be inaccessible and unresponsive.

When the love is genuine the attachment is there and never goes away until death separates one from the other. Often times the one left alone is unresponsive to others.

Separation distress is tied to strong, fundamental needs; it often elicits strong fight or flight responses. When we protect ourselves through fight or flight, we may alarm our attachment figure, who no longer sees us as providing a secure emotional base. If the attachment figure then withdraws, it confirms fear of abandonment and betrayal. Put it another way, we may blame the attachment figure for not being responsive to our needs; he or she then becomes the enemy, the betrayer. Anger, resentment, and depression may cause a further rift between us and our attachment figure.

The results, we head for the streets to the other woman to the other man and the age old scenario is birthed or continues to reap havoc;

"The Gift Women give a-way and Men buy"

From the attachment figures point of view, there is no apparent reason for us to feel either depressed or angry; these reactions seem puzzling an unreasonable. Thus as understanding and communications are eroded, the mutual satisfaction that has characterized the relationship lessens.

When a man loves a woman, can't keep his mind on nothing else, he'll tell the world, about the good thing he found. If she is bad, he can see it. Turn his back on his best friend if she put him down.

Chapter 7

LOVE AND SEX

Research indicates that women disclose more to casual acquaintances than do men. This is not surprising, since in our culture girls and women have traditionally been encouraged to share their feelings, whereas boys and men have traditionally been expected to hide their emotion. Women place emphasis on talking and emotional sharing in their relationships, whereas men tend to emphasize shared activities and limit their conversation chiefly to sports, money and sex. **(Hartfield and Rapson 1994; Tanner 1990, 1994)**

Men and women differ very little in their willingness to confide in the other. Even in deeply intimate relationships men and women differ in the kinds of things they talk about.

Communications is the central key in all relationships if you aren't communicating something is wrong and it needs attention immediately.

When there is no talking, no touching, no sitting together, or the avoidance of the appearance, we are here together; there is no trust, no respect.

It is not unusual for a battered partner to feel continued attachment to the batterer. Battered wives may also feel attachment to their batterer, a puzzling phenomenon to an outside observer; **"Why don't she just simply leave him?"** Such loyalty and persistence of attachments in the face of abuse is beyond comprehension.

Romantic love is Visionary, imaginative and adventurous. It is the idealization of beauty, grace, and charm in the woman and strength, courage, and sacrifice in the man. Romantic love is now culturally acceptable for sexual fulfillment as a component of contemporary love in our society today.

The modern concept of Romantic Love has assumed enormous importance in <u>dating</u> and <u>Relationship,</u> and it had become the major reason for marrying. Two people are expected to marry because they are in love. To be truthful with you, a lot of the time it's <u>Infatuation</u> of pure lust for what you think to be grandeur.

Modern-Day American society makes Romantic Love a primary basis for marriage and sets up the expectation that a married person will derive all Romantic satisfaction within the framework of marriage. If extra marital romantic involvement does occur, our cultural expectation is that it must either be discontinued or institutionalized through divorce or remarriage.

"The Gift Women give-a-way and Men buy"

Are Men or Women more Romantic?

Women are usually portrayed as being more romantic than men, as dreaming more often about romantic fulfillment. Women are considered to be more interested in discussing affairs of the heart, whereas men are traditionally expected to talk about such things as sports, cars, and business.

We are living in a changing world and marriage has changed as well. What's wrong with treating her, your wife, the way you did before you said "I do?" No more dinners out, no movies, no flowers, no more special nights just you and I. It's because of the smell of the other woman's perfume has garnered your attention totally. If you love that smell why not buy the same for your wife.

Romantic Love, sex, and marriage are intreging subjects and still are today.

Our modern concept of Romantic Love originated in the twelfth (12th) Century as **Courtly Love,** which was embodied in the devotion of an errant knight who swore eternal fealty (Fidelity) loyalty, and devotion to his lady. Courtly Love was always sexual. Sex was regarded as ignoble, degrading, and animalistic. Proper chivalrous conduct demanded that there be no sexual relations between a Courtly Lover and his lady.

A knight's love for his lady was expected to exemplify the platonic ideal of selfless courage and sacrifice without any physical contact and often without any communication what so ever.

If that was ideal today, marriages would be even farther away from each other.

When we can't get what we want today, what do we do? We turn to the other woman, the other man.

Love and Sex

Sex, that is overt sex or sexual interaction, may or may not be a part of passionate or romantic love within a couple. In other words, it's possible that sex is not at all part of a romantic relationship. It is of moderate importance or is of central importance to one or both members of a couple. If sex is of central importance to the couple, it may add an explosive dimension to their emotional involvement with each other, but the question remains, **where is God in this marriage? In this sexual relationship between this un-married couple? God has been left out and so goes the ideal of a marriage built on the principles of Christ.**

Love is a commitment for the two to respect, cherish, and honor one another.

Infatuation is commonly understood to mean a foolish fatuous, extravagant passion or attachment. It is typically used to distinguish an emotion that may seem like love, but is not love, even though it has the characteristics of romantic or passionate love.

The decision to marry has far reaching consequences, for it will irrevocably change the rest of a person's life.

Why do we choose to marry instead of cohabiting, obtaining the benefits of marriage without the responsibilities.

The Spouse with more education tends to be more dominant in the marriage, whether lower or middle class. The spouse with the greater verbal skills, who is relatively fluent in talking and persuading, tends to be dominant in the marriage, lower or middle class. A marriage needs to be based on mutuality, and not on one's force of the other to do as I say.

Marital Interaction and Sex

Dreams among the most important parts of marriage are companionship; intimacy; shared thought, plans, and dreams; enjoyable leisure time together; high quality communication with each other; and religious fulfillment. Sex is also one of the key aspects of marriage. What is important is not the extent of sexual activity, but that each have about the same level of sexual interest and responsiveness, or that the spouse with the lower sex drive take pleasure in pleasing the other.

Sex affects almost every aspect of a couple's interaction and that **"A good sex life is central to a good overall relationship in most marriages"**

Nearly half of the married couples in society copulated three or more time a week during the first ten years of marriage. After ten or more years, they copulate two or three times a week, if not less. For most couples with marital problems, frequency and regularity of copulation were positively correlated with the level of happiness in the marriage.

Who initiates and who complies?

For a wife to demand compliance from her husband is much less common than for her husband to demand sexual compliance from his wife. This pattern results from the long-held tradition in our Society that men initiate sexual activity, where women comply. Because of this expectation, it may be risky for a wife to demand sexual compliance from her husband.

The use of Sex for Power

According to the principles of least interest, a wife who is less interested in sex than her husband, can use sex as a weapon, withholding it as punishment and granting it as a favor, to control her husband and manipulate power. A man does not have that kind of power over the woman and rarely use that as a tactic. A husband is more apt to use sex as a demonstration of power by simply demanding sexual compliance from a reluctant wife. These terms leave a marriage in jeopardy of falling apart.

Women marry believing that their husbands will change; men marry believing that their wives will not change. They are both wrong. The problem is the outside influences.

When you are a married man, you don't need to be away from your wife and hanging out with your boys, or in the club or bar. Who are you looking for? Do you not have what God joined you with? Are you not satisfied?

Your friends introduce you to one of their friend's girls and a casual conversation sparks an interest and soon you meet again, but this time, just the two of you and you share a meal together, she eats out of your plate and you out of hers. A slip of hands causes you to touch her hand or she touches yours. You walk her to her car and a simple hug becomes a small kiss that evolves into an affair, and soon, as a married man, you have begun your first extra-marital relationship. You liked what you just did because if you didn't, you would not be anxious to do it again.

She begins to bring food on your job for you. People see her and know she is not your wife and soon the talk begins.

Your car has been seen in her driveway. Her kids know you in public and your wife begins to wonder why.

The age old expression; **"What's done in the dark will be shown in the light"** comes true in this instance.

We as men wonder why the <u>good girl</u> we have at home has now begun to run the street a little herself. It's because she has put up with your women calling, hearing about your affairs, no money in your pockets for your family, because you have spent it on your other woman. **"When a woman is fed up, there isn't anything you can do about it."**

Every man wants a great woman in his life and he does everything right to get her. We want that special somebody that we can take home and show off to mom and dad, your friends and best buddy. We want a lady of class, culture and beauty. We want a lady who has charm, poise, personality, and has the superior degree of femininity. She is a lady who goes to church, comes from a good family, educated and yet you drive her from all the above, into the arms of another man.

"What's this whole world coming to; things just aren't the same, when the hunter gets captured by the game".

Now that we have this darling of a lady in our lives, she has given you children, she is always at a church service with the children, she has a few pounds more, you stay on her last nerve because you run the streets, and yet you will not keep a job. She pays the house note, the utility bill, buys the groceries, pays the car note, you steal from her purse to buy alcohol and drugs, to give to your other woman, and you come home looking like a **Bum**, smelling like another woman's perfume, and you expect her to submit to your every command, do you think that's right? We married a human being and she has feelings also.

<u>The Conflict</u>

The challenge is to avoid as many conflicts ad possible, to reduce the chances of them re-occurring. If conflicts occur to often or if they are allowed to persist, mount-up, strengthen, the greater the dissension conflicts can ruin a relationship, destroy harmony, pleasure, contentment, and delight will be replaced by pure bitterness and soon hate. Hate can and will take you to a degree of contemplating doing something drastic to your partner/mate.

Conflicts that occur within an intimate relationship are ironically more likely to escalate than a social conflict.

Conflict in a marriage is inevitable and unavoidable. The interactions and characteristics of marriage, sooner or later, one will want something that the other does not want at the time. Conflicts are more often in a marriage than in dating because **the** two people who are dating find that they do not want the same thing at the same time, they are likely to simply stop dating. **"Honesty and Communication are the keys to open up the channels of conflict."** Once a couple decides to marry, they are held together, **by the bonds of matrimony hopefully,** because it is more difficult to end a marriage than to stop dating. You are forced to confront the conflict within the relationship and to deal with it, one way or another. If Christ be in it, the conflict can and will be resolved. If the situation is all you had for me, greater problems may exist than you could ever imagine.

The complexity of some situations can play out by one wanting his or her way. Let's look at a situation where the husband wants a window open but the wife wants the window closed. In response, the wife may then be disinclined to make love and in refusing to do so establishes a **"win"** in this area of their relationship. Is it worth it for the husband to have the window open? If his win in this situation will cause a disintegration of another aspect of their relationship. This is a complexed question. We are inclined to resolve the conflict in a harmonious way rather than allow it to become destructive. Sooner or later, this type of behavior will force him to go elsewhere if he hasn't been going already.

"The Gift Women Give-A-Way And Men Buy"

Someone has to give in this time with no strings attached, and the next time the other spouse should bow in without stipulation. Men force some women to go out and do the very same thing. It is wrong; it is sin no matter which one does it. Your body is hers and hers is yours for the sexual gratification in your marriage. It is so perverted that we have no morals in society today. We will lay with anyone who will consent and get up and go home to lay with him or her like we have done nothing wrong.

When either of us knows we are guilty, we will usually respond to the conflict with either **reality – oriented behavior** or **defense-oriented behavior.** Behavior that is directed toward obtaining the satisfaction that one is being denied is called; **Reality-Oriented Behavior.** Behavior that is not directed towards obtaining this satisfaction but instead either lowers tension related to dissatisfaction or lowers tension by acting to obtain substitute satisfaction is called **Defense – Oriented Behavior.**

Most married couples and most of Society are unaware of the following;

"God doesn't give us what we can handle; He helps us, handle what we have been given."

We profess to be able to handle situations on the streets, in our family business, but we are unable to handle our households. How can God use a man who has trouble handling his own house hold?

We are allowing too much to go unnoticed in the home, in the relationship with you and your spouse, and allowing **SPIRITUAL FORNICATION** to become rambunctious. Anytime we think it's alright for a married man or married woman to meet in the Church for a Sexual Rendezvous after Service, after Bible Study, after Choir Rehearsal, after any Church related activity, it constitutes fornication in the Church, knowingly or unknowingly.

This is a conflict when the wife knows it, or the husband knows it, and has related it to the Church, but it has not been addressed. Why? Because often time we as leaders have been the source of the conflict, fornication in the Church. The reason I call it spiritual fornication in the church, is because it has been done in the name of Jesus. We have told a lie and the truth ain't in us.

In marriage, reality – oriented behavior requires, first, an attempt to get a clear perspective on the problem at hand, and second, an attack on the problem, not on the other person, an attack on the other person might score a **"Win"** but undermines the overall harmony of the relationship.

The ways people attack the other person in a conflict, rather than attacking the source of the conflict, tend to follow certain patterns, for certain ethnicities depending on the personalities of the individuals. Some people tend to be authoritarian, whereas others tend to be passive or evasive. These patterns of attack tend to fall into categories that can be described as authoritarian resolution permissive acceptance, passive aggression, evasion, blaming, placating, distracting, and computing.

Some people are permissive, they give in. Authoritarian are probably the common method of resolving a conflict. Passive is a method of resolving a conflict that resembles permissive acceptance, but is actually very aggressive. Evasion is a pattern of coping with the conflict that is similar to passive aggression.

Frustration is the emotion experienced when an important need is being blocked or when an important satisfaction is being denied. The most common felt effect of a conflict is the frustration experienced by both people in the relationship, but felt especially keenly by the person who feels most deprived in the situation. Sometimes both parties may feel the same dissatisfaction.

A common frustration in today's Society for married couples and those living together occurs when one wishes to have sex and the other person refuses.

There are times as married couples that you have to give in to the other for the sake of conflict resolution.

Chapter 8

WHY DO I DO THE THINGS I DO?

Why do I do the things I do? Why do I go after something that's not ordained by God for me to have?

Your spouse has fear of STD's from you because she knows that you are sexually active outside the marriage. Take her out of the fear of this by staying at home.

Women are more likely than a man to acquire an STD from a single sexual encounter. A woman's risk of infection from a STD causes her to suffer more long-term consequences than men. She may suffer infertility, chronic pelvic pain, cervical cancer, and they are less likely to have early symptoms of the disease. They are less likely to seek early Health Care for an STD.

As men, we are naughty by nature. A woman can lead a man into many a situation by the promise of her gift. Then there are others who will not venture to promise or to share it with no man until the bonds of matrimony have been rightfully sealed. Those kind are hard to find, but they are out there, ask me I know.

From the beginning of time and even now, man has been seduced by woman when he realized the gift she had and what it could do for him. That gift led Adam to eat of the forbidden fruit, Sampson to do what Delilah told him to do, Hosea to go and get Gomer back after she had left him with two sons that were not his and gone off with other men. It has caused men to lose their lives by taking it themselves because she has left them and it has caused men to lose their minds and their sanity.

But, because of our sinful nature, we want more than what God has given us and that nature destroys great marriages, beautiful homes, splits families, displaces children's, brings down an institution built by God, the Church, rocks the core of businesses and completely demolishes a political career. Why? Because we are naughty by nature. It's just in us.

Revelations 3:15 say

"I know your works, that you are neither cold nor hot, I would you were cold or hot."

We will cross every tee and dot every eye, dress-up, change our way of talking, acting, and even go to church to win her affection, her time, and her consideration. Ninety (90%) per cent of the time, if he receives the gift to soon, or before marriage, he has already begun an extra-curricular affair.

A lot of men blame the woman for their force to the other woman. If that is your excuse, it's weak and shallow.

We have the resource to keep the fire burning (raging) in our marriage. Whatever it was you were doing prior to marriage pleasing in the sight of God, continue so the flame never goes out.

Well I try, but she is always so tired. You have to do things that makes her feel compelled to give you the gift. You running the streets all night, not sharing the household responsibilities, no flowers, no candy, no movie night, what about a dinner date, but you expect her to roll-over and just give-in, treat her like a lady and you will see a different attitude.

You take your outside woman out shopping, pay her car note, and give her kids money, but what about your own home situation? The answer is, we have left God out.

What God has joined together, let no man put asunder.

There is no need to become angry and bitter to the point of leaving the house. Sooner or later you are going to return. But, if you are lukewarm, the enemy will convince you to go to the other woman's house.

When you were dating, before marriage, not during marriage, it was for companionship, fun, adventure, romance, and sometimes sex. You have all of that now at home in your marriage.

It's just in our nature to be sinful when it comes to sexual gratification. When does it stop? Where does it stop? When a doctor has told you that you are HIV positive? You have less than six months to live? How do you go back home and tell your wife who has been faithful to you for over twenty years, had never known no other man but you, how and what do you tell your children? Your church members? your neighbors? Your friends?

There is a story I am reminded of that shows a man in his hunting apparel in the woods hunting for a deer. He disappears out of sight, and you hear a gunshot. A few minutes go by and you see the deer dressed in the hunter's clothes, the rifle across his shoulder pulling the hunter out of the woods.

The moral behind this is;

"What's this whole world coming to; things just aren't the same, anytime the hunter gets captured by the Game.

Ask her;

Where do you and I go from here?

The Bible does say that marriage is an oneness, a joining together, a uniting together, but it's more than that. It is a uniting together by a covenant. The word **"Covenant"** In Hebrew is **Berith,** and it has the ideal of binding together. It's a final commitment of an individual, even commitment until death does part you. If you went into a Harlot, such an evil sin as that, there would be no commitment on your part to her. The essence of marriage is to first of all forsake all others. It's forsaking all others for this one, to commit yourself to one.

If we don't honor and appreciate our wives as being the weaker vessel and realize that we are heirs together of the grace of life, our prayers will be hindered. (1 Peter 3:7).

Marriage is a serious thing. Love is the ruling principle in marriage, and our spiritual lives could be hindered if we do not walk in the unity and harmony that God has designed for the marriage relationship. This is a Covenant we make to an individual, but it's also a covenant that we make before God. God has a priority that is for us to focus on our marriage

Matthew 7:12 say's;

Therefore all things whatsoever you would that men should do to you, do you even so to them, for this is the law and prophets.

This is just the exact principle that should rule in our marriages. It is not a selfish thing, not for self, not about what this person can give you.

The reason marriage is designed the way it is, is because it is an example, a model, and as a real relationship with Christ should be. He has given us illustrations in the natural, He has shown us how to have a great marriage, a good marriage, and because He wants us to have a model of what a real eternal relationship is to be with him. Marriage is a merger not just a partnership. You have to assure her of all of the above.

Where our problem comes in at is, we have to

appreciate our mate, we put her down, we talk to her any type of way in public, in the presence of family and friends, and we disrespect her by not holding her hand in high esteem anywhere, everywhere. You were at one time proud to hold her hand and now that she is your wife, you have to continue to, **treat her like your lady.**

When you speak words over your spouse, they will rise to the level of the words you speak. but, if you say, **you are no good, you are ugly, you need to fix your hair, you are overweight,"** you will suppress your marriage and not cause oneness but separation and alienation, but when you speak words of kindness like; **Honey, I appreciate the things you do, I appreciate you, I love you so much",** and back the words up with action, your spouse/mate will rise up to the level of those words.

Can't you see today that a lot of the problems in our marriages are the words spoken, you have brought your spouse/mate down instead of up. A lot of women are guilty of this problem as well. When you tell a man that he is no good and will never be a real man that destroys his desire to do better, to show his manhood or to operate in his leadership role as head of the household. If he is not working because he has been laid off but he seeks to find employment, stand by your man, and you stand by your woman, because you will need each other and your family needs you both.

Begin today with acts of kindness, just like painting several coats of lacquer on a piece of finished wood that's how love is built. I wish I had practiced these lessons years ago. Like so many even today we have had to experience what I am going through now to fully understand the meaning; **"You never miss your water until your well runs dry."**

Strangely enough, when we are dating that lady trying to win her heart, we have never forgotten her birthday, the anniversary of the two of you meeting for the first time. The little things she likes and the places she like to go. As soon as the element of surprise is over, she is no longer our top priority.

Go back to the drawing board, seek the information you need to restore your marriage to its beginning.

Despite its importance in marriage and in the family, the subject of money is often cloaked in mystery. The subject of money and sex are twin areas of ignorance and ineptness in our society today. A man will spend his last dollar, the rent payment, the grocery bill, for a high and the thrill of being with a woman. Most men know less about money than they do themselves.

A man who really desires to get **his wife** back into **his arms** has to have God in his life as the central control.

Wine or Liquor won't do it. Physical abuse will not do it. Force will not accomplish or complete your plan or re-structure. You need help.

You need not only show real love, but you need to prove and demonstrate such love.

LOVE

<u>Eros;</u>	is a breath taking experience you have when you meet her and she is the one, the special one;
<u>Ludus</u>	You experience love as an affair for amusement, or pleasure;
<u>Manic</u>	A love feeling one gets from a song, lyrics, plays, operas, ballets, or a romantic novel;
<u>Storge</u>	This is an unexciting, non-passionate form of love;
<u>Pragma</u>	Is a practical logical love closely related to storge;
<u>Agape</u>	It is an altruistic, spiritual love. Some degree of agape, or altruism, is probably a necessary ingredient for any type of lasting love with in a marriage.

In order for it to work you need favor with God. You need to seek his counseling and allow him to give you the words to say to your wife.

<u>Proverb 12:2 say's;</u>

<u>A good man obtains favor of The Lord, but a man of wicked devices will he condemn.</u>

Favor of the Lord is the highest attainment of any seeker. It is stated that only a **"Good Man"** can secure such; however the **"Goodness"** is only that which God gives.

That's where you go from here.

<u>"The Gift Women Give-A-Way and Men Buy"</u>

SERMON

Text: <u>St. John 8:1-11</u>

(1) **Jesus went unto the Mount of Olives,**

(2) **And early in that morning He came again into the temple, and all the people came unto Him; And he sat down, and taught them.**

(3) **And the Scribes and Pharisees brought unto him a woman taken in adultery; and when they had set her in the midst.**

(4) **They say unto Him, Master this woman was taken in adultery, in the very act,**

(5) **Now Moses in the Law commanded us, that such should be stoned; but what sayest thou**

(6) **This they said, tempting him, that they might have to accuse him, but Jesus stooped down, and with his finger wrote on the ground, as though he heard them not.**

(7) **So when they continued asking him, he lifted up himself, and said unto them, he who is without sin among you, let him first cast a stone at her.**

(8) **And again he stooped down, and wrote on the ground,**

(9) **And they which heard it, being convicted by their own conscience went out one by one, beginning at the eldest, even unto the last: and Jesus was left alone, and the woman standing in the midst.**

(10) **When Jesus had lifted up himself, and saw none but the woman, where are those your accuses? Has no man condemned you?**

(11) **She said, no man Lord, and Jesus said unto her, neither do I condemn you: Go and sin no more.**

Subject: "<u>You Can See Me, But You Can't See Yourself</u>".

The writer of this Gospel was the Apostle John, who also wrote the Epistles of John, and Revelation. This may have been the last of the Gospels to be written, probably about A.D. 90. John, a Fisherman of Galilee, Son of Zebedee and brother of James, was dearly loved by the Lord, for He sat next to Him at the last supper, and He calls himself **One Whom Jesus loved.**

The law was given by God to Moses for the Jewish people to observe. It was just and right and it demanded that all wrongdoings should be punished. It showed God's Holiness and justice, but it could never save people, for they could not keep it perfectly. While God has always been gracious, His grace was perfectly demonstrated through the death of His son in the sinner's place. Thus, grace came by Jesus Christ.

No man has seen God. No man can see God, because He is a spirit and has no bodily form. When God wanted to speak to men in the Old Testament times, He took a body or appeared in a flame of fire or in a bright cloud. Men did not see Him, Just the outward form. People could not even come near to God when He did reveal Himself like this, because they were sinful, but the Lord Jesus Christ took a human body and lived in this world, and through His perfect life, His love, and His goodness, people saw God and what He is like.

Let's interject right here, a true Notation;

<u>"Religion may keep you out of Jail, but only The Blood of Jesus, will keep you out of Hell"</u>

Some Folk believe that their Religious-osity is all they need to get into Heaven. You see, your religion may be a stumbling block in someone else way. You people/we people, think it's all about us. Your task is to seek the truth. The folk you think are going to Hell may not be there, and the folk you think are going to Heaven, may not be there. ("I wish I had a praying Church, say Yeah!!!)

Most of us tend to live in a way that draws attention to ourselves, our clothes, our careers, our positions, our cleverness, our success, and when life is all about us, it's hard for people to see Jesus in us. Jesus saved us to be reflections of His glory, but when we live for ourselves; our shadow gets cast upon the canvas of His presence in us. A Christians Life is the canvas on which others can see Jesus.

According to our scripture, Jesus went out to the Mount of Olives, early in the morning and many people came unto Him.

Up pops the Scribes and the Pharisees, the Religious folk. In today's times, they would be considered the suddities, The Debutants, The Scholars, The People of Class; abruptly bringing the adulterous woman into the midst of the proceedings was a rude disruption. The Pharisees were bent on confounding Jesus.

The law had already been broken in addition to the offense, by them bringing the woman without the man.

"You can See Me, But You can't See Yourself"

Why were they or had they intended to punish the woman but not the man? The pronoun **YOU** is emphatic. The Religious leaders were trying to trap Jesus into saying something that would hold Jesus contrary to the Law.

They were unaware that He was The Son of The Law Giver.

If Jesus would have said not to stone her, He would have contradicted Jewish Law. If He had said to stone her, He would have run counter to Roman's Law, which did not permit them to carry out their own executions. What Jesus **wrote on the ground** is a matter of conjecture. Some suggested that He wrote the Ten Commandments recorded in Exodus 20. Had the content of His writing been critical, it would have been recorded. Perhaps, the issue was not the content of what He wrote but the act of writing. In The Old Testament, God wrote The Law with His fingers. Maybe by writing the law Jesus is symbolically saying He is not the teacher of the Law; He is the giver of the Law. If He were merely a Rabbi, He would only assert the Mosaic Prescription of Judgment. As The Giver of the law, He could do for this woman what God had done for Israel at Sinai-; He could forgive.

This scene could have happened in a few minutes. Thus, as this all happened the Sun was rising. As the Sun sheds it's light, their guilty past was exposed by The Light of the World.

Verse eleven (11) say's; <u>Sin No More</u> implies that Jesus forgave her. He did not condemn her, but neither did He Condone her sin. Some think that the Lord will forgive them after they have done the best they can. Jesus forgave this woman after she did the worse she could. Jesus loves us just the way we are, but loves us too much to leave us that way.

Some of us think that we are the most Holiest of all and believe we can do whatever we want and still be in God's good graces. Folk think they can run with the wolves, and lay with the Lambs. They see everything you and I do, but slip and slide, hide behind closed doors, and think they aren't visible when they come out of their place of sinfulness.

Some Folk can always criticize the other, but what about you? If walls could really talk, they would tell the stories on so many of us, and our ungodly behaviors and those with us.

"You can see Me, But You Can't See Yourself"

In 2ⁿᵈ. Kings 20ᵗʰ Chapter, Verses One thru six 1-6).

1. In those days were Hezekiah sick unto death, and the Prophet Isaiah the Son of Amos came to him, and said unto him, thus saith the Lord, "Set thine house in order; for thou shalt die, and not live.
2. Then he turned his face to the wall, and prayed unto the Lord saying,
3. I beseech thee, O Lord, remember now how I have walked before thee in truth and with a perfect heart, and have done that which is good in thy sight, and Hezekiah wept sore.
4. And it came to pass, before Isaiah was gone out into the middle Court, that the word of the Lord came to him saying,
5. Turn again, and tell Hezekiah the Captain of my people, thus saith the Lord, the God of David thy father. I have heard thy prayer, I have seen thy tears; behold I will heal thee; on the third day thou shalt go up unto the House of the Lord.

6. And I will add unto thy days fifteen years; and I will deliver thee and this City out of the hand of the King of Assyria;

Keep praying no matter what you are going through, and God will hear and answer your sincere prayer.

Anytime we profess to be Christians, full of the Spirit, living so righteously, we say, and have a girlfriend, a wife at home, a boyfriend, a husband at home, or chasing another man or chasing another woman, then there is something wrong with our Christianity. Your body, your flesh, has not received the news that you are different; you are a new creature in Christ. The only thing new is the Woman you spent two or three nights a week with, or that thundering, chiseled man you see every day before going home to your husband., Oh!! If walls could talk, some of us right here, right how, would get up and tip out with that one finger up.

"You Can See Me, but You Can't See Yourself"

I heard a saying that say's:

"You must be careful who you lay down with, because it might not be as easy as you think to get-up and walk away."

What's done in the dark will surely come to the light when you least expect it. You may be on one of your extra marital excursions, and run into someone that you esteem the highest, and they may esteem you the highest, and you both, you discover, are hiding from one another.

God is sick and tired of our mess and our justification for what we know is wrong. Every man his own wife, and every wife her own husband. Folks don't care whether you see them or not anymore. It's my thing. I'll do like I want to do. It's your body, but your body is the temple of God and you can't put anything in it. I wish you could see the importance of the words I just told you. If you are living in a glass house, don't throw any stones.

"You can see Me, But You Can't See Yourself"

The blame was placed on the sinning woman, but according to the twentieth (20th) chapter of Leviticus and the tenth (10th) verse, it says;

And the man that committed adultery with another man's wife, even he that committed adultery with his neighbor's wife, the **Adulterer** and the **Adulteress** shall surely be put to death; and

St. John 8th chapter, Verse 5 (five) say's;

Moses in the Law, both the **Adulteress** and the **Adulterer** should have been arrested – not just the woman. According to the Law, both would have been stoned. The leaders were again trying to trap Jesus.

Sin will lead you down the Pole of nothingness, quicker than oil on the Pole sliding down.

How Does Sin Start?

For a man or a woman, like in our Scripture read into your hearing, Sin is first.

1. **Observation:** Unrighteous exposure, our attempts to entertain stuff that we should not. She looks good, he looks good, that dress looks good on her, and that suit looks good on him, and;
2. **Toleration:** Acceptance which dulls our Spiritual Life. God has given you a wife or a husband and now you want to tolerate the lust, the demonic spirit, that has ruined your Christian Life with just a few minutes pleasure, and;
3. **Admiration:** Starts to look good, so now you are paying compliments, paying bills buying flowers, making house payments and rent payments, you are all in now. There is no turning back, I like what I see I'll be the other man for what I see, and;
4. **Experimentation:** We will lower our standards of expectation just for the fact of being with this one particular woman. She may not look as good as your wife, he may not look as good and

handsome as your husband, but something about them makes you wild enough to risk your marriage. Your family status, but most of all your relationship with Christ, and;

5. **Participation:** Total loss of Sensitivity to the right to justify this misdeed, this violation of your vows, your wanting to spend all night with this person who is not yours, will not be yours, and has no desire to be yours. They only want a good time with some fringe benefits.

6. **"You Can See Me, but You Can't See Yourself"**

7. **Justification:** You will make excuses for the foolishness by saying; he drove me into the arms of another man. She pushed me out into the streets and now I can't stay away from her, from him. You continue to live a lie, acting the part of a husband at home, and / or acting the part of a loving wife at home. You don't know how your family is affected by your extra-marital affairs.

8. **Consummation:** Totally consumed. You are controlled by this things behavior. Now you are so into this behavior that you don't care who sees you, your children, friends or whomever. You have thrown your bit of religion over your shoulder and total disrespect is shown to your marriage partner. You won't go to church with your family, but you will show up with your baby mama, your baby daddy, and even got the nerve to shout; what are you shouting about? When you hear Christ condemning sexual activity, that's because it's out of the realms of matrimony.

Let's look at our Scripture now, and the story being illustrated.

The King James Version of the Bible denotes this chapter by caption. That say's;

"The Sinning Woman" The Scribes and the Pharisees, The Historically self-righteous and Public Clerk of Society, came to Jesus and began to tell Him about the sinning woman. Notice now, they did not bring the man. To be accused of the Act she was tagged with, she needed a willing partner. In those days she needed a man. In today's realm, she could have been w/ another woman, but the point I'm trying to get you to see is, folk are always taking someone else's business and making it public. If the truth is to be told, "All have sinned and come short of the Glory of God."

Haven't you seen folk who are so righteous and profess to live so close to God and when their secret is publicized they commit suicide, or they lose their mind.

"You can see Me, But You Can't See Yourself"

Let me show you at least one situation that illustrates why we should put the wrongdoings of another in God's hands.

Acts the ninth chapter, verses thirthteen through sixteen says:

Then Ananias answered, Lord I have heard by many of this man, how much evil he hath done to thy saints at, Jerusalem.

And here He hath authority from the Chief priests to bind all that call on thy name.

But the Lord said unto him, go thy way; for he is a chosen vessel unto me to bear my name before the Gentiles, and Kings, and the Children of Israel;

For I will show Him how great things he must suffer for my names sake.

Ananias you can see Saul but you can't see yourself. Great God almighty, I feel my company keeper has arrived and I'm ready to preach, now.

Please, allow me to use my imagination as the Spirit leads me. As the high-society folk came to Jesus and began to run this woman down. They asked the question, Moses in the law commanded us, that such should be stoned, but what sayest thou?

Jesus stooped down, and with His finger He wrote on the ground, as though He heard them not.

They kept asking Him; what they should do. He lifted up Himself, and said unto them. "He that is without sin among you, let him first cast a stone at her."

And again He stooped down, and wrote on the ground. Thank God for His favor when you live by His word truthfully.

"You Can See Me, But You can't See Yourself."

Ananias thought that because Saul had persecuted the Christians, had been in a Roman Jail, had been an outcast in his community, didn't have fine clothes to wear, didn't drive a Benz, didn't have a $500,000.00 home, little did Ananias know that God specializes in cleaning up a mess. Note if you will, Jesus said, "Go Thy Way," in other words, Ananias go do what I told you to do, and don't worry about his past, it's in my hands and so is his future.

Can't you see Jesus telling the Scribes and Pharisees, who among you has the nerve to cast/throw the first stone at this woman, at this man? I wish I had somebody ready and willing to give God some praise.

"You Can See Me, but You Can't See Yourself"

I'm coming in soon, but what I like most about our scripture is the bottom of verse ten:

Jesus said; Accusers? Hath no man condemned thee? She said, no man Lord, and Jesus said unto her, neither do I condemn thee, Go, and sin no more."

We are living in a mean, wicked and torned world. Folk don't have any morals now days. There is a dissimulation in family life. We are falling away from God. There is husband against wife, wife against husband, children disobeying their parents and even killing them. Our School systems are no longer graduating Little Scholars, but Little Gangsters, and Little Prostitutes. Teachers are being run out of the classrooms by students with guns of mass destruction. Self-Respect has evaporated the Milk of

Human kindness, pain and panic chase each other like June Bugs in the Summer Sun. People just don't want to do right. People are raising hell everywhere. There are shootings in the Courtroom, in the emergency room at the Hospital, in the Funeral Home parking lots, in the Church services and most anywhere now days. We are falling away from God.

I remember when folk wouldn't go into a Church parking Lot to drink Beer, but now they will drink whiskey, Beer or wine in there while the Pastor is preaching. Folk just won't do right, Preachers won't do right, Church members won't do right, and the People of God won't do right. Why? Because we think we can do anything and others will not see us. God sees all and knows all.

"You Can See Me, but You Can't See Yourself"

You and her know right from wrong and when a married man, a married woman, a man with another man or a woman with another woman, God knows all about it. You don't have to hide from the world. Your sins will tell on you. Your fervor in your preaching and praying will diminish, your luster in your marriage will soon die out. God is sick and tired of us playing games.

NOTE

No one has to look over you or me to see if we will do right. That internal regulator makes you and I do right. Sometimes vines have to be pruned and so it is with our lives.

I may have slept in a Garage, but that doesn't make me a Car. I may have slept with the Chickens, but that doesn't make me a Chicken.

Whatever tomb you may have been in or feel someone has placed you in; the Angels are ready to Roll back the Curtains.

Those things that I love, I hold dear to my heart, I just borrowed them. They are not mines at all. Jesus only let me use them to brighten up my life. So remind me, remind me dear Lord.

Nothing good that I've done. I don't deserve God's only Son. I'm not worthy of the nails in His hand.

Why He chose the road to Calvary, just to die instead, why He loves me, I just can't understand. So roll back the curtains of memory now and then, Lord show me where you brought me from, and where I could have been, remember that I am only human, and as humans we forget, so remind me, remind me, dear Lord.

"You Can See Me, but You Can't See Yourself"

He is not Pack Man; you cannot bump Him around to suit your outside pleasures. You may have been through something that leaves you feeling like God can't use you.

Don't you quit and don't you give up

Don't quit when the Tide is lowest

For it's just about to turn;

Don't quit over doubts and questions

For there's something you may learn.

Don't quit when the Night is darkest.

For it's just a while till dawn;

Don't quit when you've run the farthest,

For the race is almost won

Don't quit when the Hill is steepest,

For your goal is almost nigh;

Don't quit for you're almost nigh;

Don't quit for you're not a failure

Until you fail to try.

The words of Jesus Christ spoken into my heart have made me a new Man/Woman so don't quit do the right thing. Live by God's Word and command.

WHO DAT?

AFTER A LONG NIGHT OF LOVE MAKING, THE GUY NOTICED A PHOTO OF ANOTHER MAN ON THE WOMAN'S NIGHTSTAND BY THE BED. HE BEGAN TO WORRY. IS THIS YOUR HUSBAND? HE NERVOUSLY ASKS. "NO SILLY, SHE REPLIED, SNUGGLING UP TO HIM. YOUR BOYFRIEND THEN? HE CONTINUES.

NO; NOT AT ALL SHE SAY'S NIBBLING AWAY AT HIS EAR. IS IT YOUR DAD OR YOUR BROTHER? HE INQUIRES, HOPING TO BE ASSURED. NO. NO. NO.? YOU ARE SO HOT WHEN YOU'RE JEALOUS, SHE ANSWERS.

SHE WHISPERS IN HIS EAR, THAT'S ME BEFORE THE SURGERY............

ISN'T IT STRANGE HOW WE AS MEN, HAVE BEEN OUT AND LAID WITH DIFFERENT WOMEN OTHER THAN OUR SPOUSE! I WONDER IF ANY OF US HAVE EXPERIENCE ANY OF THE ABOVE? HOW MANY HAVE WENT BACK HOME AND HAVE GOTTEN SEXUALLY INVOLVED WITH YOUR SPOUSE AND NEVER SAFEGUARDED YOURSELF OR THAT LOVE ONE? **YOU CAN EXHALE NOW!**

Printed in the United States
By Bookmasters